EVERY GOOD BOY DESERVES FAVOUR
and
PROFESSIONAL FOUL

EVERY GOOD BOY DESERVES FAVOUR

A Play for Actors and Orchestra

and

PROFESSIONAL FOUL

A Play for Television

TOM STOPPARD

faber and faber

LONDON · BOSTON

First published in 1978
by Faber and Faber Limited
3 Queen Square London WC1N 3AU
Reprinted 1978, 1984 (twice) and 1986

Printed in Great Britain by
Whitstable Litho Ltd., Whitstable, Kent
All rights reserved

British Library Cataloguing in Publication Data

Stoppard, Tom
Every good boy deserves favour, and,
Professional foul.
I. Title   II. Stoppard, Tom. Professional foul
822'.9'14   PR6069.T6E/
ISBN 0-571-11225-0
ISBN 0-571-11226-9 Pbk

INTRODUCTION

Every Good Boy Deserves Favour is the title of a work of which the text is only a part. The sub-title, 'A Play for Actors and Orchestra', hardly indicates the extent to which the effectiveness of the whole depends on the music composed by André Previn. And it is to him that the work owes its existence.

As the principle conductor of the London Symphony Orchestra, Mr Previn invited me in 1974 to write something which had the need of a live full-size orchestra on stage. Invitations don't come much rarer than that, and I jumped at the chance. It turned out to be the fastest move I made on the project for the next eighteen months.

Usually, and preferably, a play originates in the author's wish to write about some particular thing. The form of the play then follows from the requirements of the subject. This time I found myself trying to make the subject follow from the requirements of the form. Mr Previn and I agreed early on that we would try to go beyond a mere recitation for the concert platform, and also that we were not writing a piece for singers. In short, it was going to be a real play, to be performed in conjunction with, and bound up with, a symphony orchestra. As far as we knew nobody had tried to do anything like that before; which, again, is not the preferred reason for starting a play, though I confess it weighed with me.

Having been given *carte blanche*, for a long time the only firm decision I was able to make was that the play would have to be in some way *about* an orchestra. For what play could escape *folie de grandeur* if it came with a hundred musicians in attendance but outside the action? And while it is next to impossible to 'justify' an orchestra, it is a simple matter to make it essential. Accordingly, I started off with a millionaire who owned one.

My difficulty in trying to make the cart pull the horse was

aggravated by the fact that I knew nothing about orchestras and very little about 'serious' music. I was in the position of a man who, never having read anything but whodunnits, finds himself writing a one-man show about Lord Byron on a *carte blanche* from an actor with a club foot. My qualifications for writing about an orchestra amounted to a spell as a triangle-player in a kindergarten percussion band. I informed my collaborator that the play was going to be about a millionaire triangle-player with his own orchestra.

This basic implausibility bred others, and at the point where the whimsical edifice was about to collapse I tried to save it by making the orchestra a mere delusion of the millionaire's brain. Once the orchestra became an imaginary orchestra, there was no need for the millionaire to be a millionaire either. I changed tack: the play would be about a lunatic triangle-player who thought he had an orchestra.

By this time the first deadline had been missed and I was making heavy weather. I had no genuine reason for writing about an orchestra, or a lunatic, and thus had nothing to write. Music and triangles led me into a punning diversion based on Euclid's axioms, but it didn't belong anywhere, and I was ready to call my own bluff.

This is where matters stood when in April 1976 I met Victor Fainberg. For some months previously I had been reading books and articles by and about the Russian dissidents, intending to use the material for a television play, and so I knew that Mr Fainberg had been one of a group of people arrested in Red Square in August 1968 during a peaceful demonstration against the Warsaw Pact invasion of Czechoslovakia. He had been pronounced insane—a not unusual fate for perfectly sane opponents of Soviet tyranny—and in 1974 he had emerged into exile from five years in the Soviet prison-hospital system. He had written about his experiences in the magazine *Index On Censorship*, an invaluable, politically disinterested monitor of political repression the world over. For Mr Fainberg freedom was, and is, mainly the freedom to double his efforts on behalf of colleagues left behind. His main concern when I met him was to secure the release of Vladimir Bukovsky, himself a victim of the abuse of psychiatry in the USSR, whose revelations about that abuse had got him sentenced to consecutive terms of prison, labour camp and internal exile amounting to twelve years.

Exceptional courage is a quality drawn from certain people in exceptional conditions. Although British society is not free of abuses, we are not used to meeting courage because conditions do not demand it (I am not thinking of the courage with which people face, say, an illness or a bereavement). Mr Fainberg's single-mindedness, his energy (drawing more on anger than on pity) and his willingness to make a nuisance of himself outside and inside the walls of any institution, friend or foe, which bore upon his cause, prompted the thought that his captors must have been quite pleased to get rid of him. He was not a man to be broken or silenced; an insistent, discordant note, one might say, in an orchestrated society.

I don't recall that I consciously made the metaphor, but very soon I was able to tell Mr Previn, definitively, that the lunatic triangle-player who thought he had an orchestra was now sharing a cell with a political prisoner. I had something to write about, and in a few weeks the play was finished.

Not that the prisoner, Alexander, is Victor or anyone else. But the speech in which he describes the treatment he received in the Leningrad Special Psychiatric Hospital is taken from the article in *Index*,* and there are other borrowings from life, such as the doctor's comment, 'Your opinions are your symptoms.' Victor Fainberg in his own identity makes an appearance in the text as one of the group 'M to S' in the speech where Alexander identifies people by letters of the alphabet.

The off-stage hero of *Every Good Boy Deserves Favour*, referred to as 'my friend C', is Vladimir Bukovsky. The Bukovsky campaign, which was supported by many people in several countries, achieved its object in December 1976, when he was taken from prison and sent to the West. In June while we were rehearsing I met Mr Bukovsky in London and invited him to call round at the Royal Shakespeare Company's rehearsal rooms in Covent Garden. He came and stayed to watch for an hour or two. He was diffident, friendly, and helpful on points of detail

* Vol. 4, no. 2, *Index on Censorship*, published by a non-profit-making company, Writers and Scholars International, 21 Russell Street, London WC2.

in the production, but his presence was disturbing. For people working on a piece of theatre, terra firma is a self-contained world even while it mimics the real one. That is the necessary condition of making theatre, and it is also our luxury. There was a sense of worlds colliding. I began to feel embarrassed. One of the actors seized up in the middle of a speech touching on the experiences of our visitor, and found it impossible to continue. But the incident was not fatal. The effect wore off, and, on the night, *Every Good Boy Deserves Favour* had recovered its nerve and its own reality.

*   *   *

The television play which I had hoped to write from the Russian material still had to be written. At least, I had promised myself that I would write a TV play to mark Amnesty International's 'Prisoner of Conscience Year' (1977), and I had promised the BBC that I would come up with something by 31st December 1976. On that day I had nothing to show, nothing begun and nothing in mind.

On 6th January in Prague three men, a playwright, an actor and a journalist, were arrested in the act of attempting to deliver a document to their own government. This document turned out to be a request that the government should implement its own laws. It pointed out that the Czechoslovak people had been deprived of rights guaranteed by an agreement made between nations at Helsinki, and that anyone who tried to claim these rights was victimized by the government which had put its name to the agreement. The document, initially signed by 241 people, was headed 'Charter 77'.

I had had ill-formed and unformed thoughts of writing about Czechoslovakia for a year or two. Moreover, I had been strongly drawn to the work and personality of the arrested playwright, Vaclav Havel. Thus it would be natural to expect that the setting and subject matter of *Professional Foul* declared themselves as soon as the Charter story broke, but in fact I was still sifting through a mass of Amnesty International documents about Russia, and when a friend invited me to keep him company on a week's visit to Moscow and Leningrad, I went hoping that the trip would unlock the play.

Perhaps predictably, the trip made the play much more difficult, since it brought me too close to the situation to leave me with any desire to trick it out with 'character', 'dramatic shape', 'dénoument', and so on, but not close enough to enable me to write about it from the inside. Instead, the trip to Russia unlocked a play about Czechoslovakia: there was an Archimedean footing, somewhere between involvement and detachment, which offered a point of leverage. By the beginning of March the general scheme of *Professional Foul* had been worked out, and after that the play was written very quickly, the first draft in about three weeks.

Meanwhile, Vaclav Havel was in gaol, on charges devised to dissociate his arrest from his activities as a spokesman for Charter 77. After four and a half months he was released, pending his trial; which took place while this Introduction was being written. For 'attempting to damage the name of the State abroad', Mr Havel was sentenced to fourteen months, suspended for two years.

He would be the first to object that in mentioning his name only, I am putting undue emphasis on his part in the Czechoslovakian human rights movement. Others have gone to gaol, and many more have been victimized. This is true. But I have in mind not just the Chartist but the author of *The Garden Party*, *The Memorandum*, *The Audience* and other plays. It is to a fellow writer that I dedicate *Professional Foul* in admiration.

EVERY GOOD BOY DESERVES FAVOUR
A Play for Actors and Orchestra

To Victor Fainberg and Vladimir Bukovsky

Characters

ALEXANDER

IVANOV

SACHA

DOCTOR

TEACHER (female)

COLONEL

Although in this edition only the text is
printed, *Every Good Boy Deserves Favour* is a
work consisting of words and music, and is
incomplete without the score composed by its
co-author André Previn.

Every Good Boy Deserves Favour was first performed at the Festival Hall in July 1977, with the London Symphony Orchestra, conducted by André Previn. The cast was as follows:

ALEXANDER	Ian McKellen
IVANOV	John Wood
SACHA	Andrew Sheldon
DOCTOR	Patrick Stewart
TEACHER	Barbara Leigh-Hunt
COLONEL	Philip Locke
Director	Trevor Nunn
Designer	Ralph Koltai

Three separate acting areas are needed.
  1. The CELL *needs two beds.*
  2. The OFFICE *needs a table and two chairs.*
  3. The SCHOOL *needs a school desk.*
These areas can be as small as possible but each has to be approachable from each of the others, and the lighting on each ought to be at least partly controllable independently of the other two and of the orchestra itself, which needless to say occupies the platform.
The CELL *is occupied by two men,* ALEXANDER *amd* IVANOV. ALEXANDER *is a political prisoner and* IVANOV *is a genuine mental patient.*
It will become clear in performance, but may well be stated now, that the orchestra for part of the time exists in the imagination of IVANOV. IVANOV *has with him an orchestral triangle.*
The OFFICE *is empty.*
In the SCHOOL *the* TEACHER *stands, and* SACHA *sits at the desk.*

   CELL
The OFFICE *and* SCHOOL *are not 'lit'. In the* CELL, ALEXANDER *and* IVANOV *sit on their respective beds. The orchestra tunes-up. The tuning-up continues normally but after a minute or two the musicians lapse into miming the tuning-up.*
Thus we have silence while the orchestra goes through the motions of tuning.
IVANOV *stands up, with his triangle and rod. The orchestra becomes immobile.*
Silence.
IVANOV *strikes the triangle, once. The orchestra starts miming a performance. He stands concentrating, listening to music which we cannot hear, and striking his triangle as and when the 'music' requires it. We only hear the triangle occasionally.* ALEXANDER *watches this—a man watching another man occasionally hitting a triangle.*

15

This probably lasts under a minute. Then, very quietly, we begin to hear what IVANOV *can hear, i.e. the orchestra becomes audible. So now his striking of the triangle begins to fit into the context which makes sense of it.*

The music builds slowly, gently. And then on a single cue the platform light level jumps up with the conductor in position and the orchestra playing fully and loudly. The triangle is a prominent part in the symphony.

Now we are flying. ALEXANDER *just keeps watching* IVANOV.

IVANOV: (*Furiously interrupts*) —No—no—no—
  (*The orchestra drags to a halt.*)
  (*Shouts.*) Go back to the timpani.
  (*The orchestra goes back, then relapses progressively, swiftly, into mime, and when it is almost inaudible* ALEXANDER *coughs loudly.* IVANOV *glances at him reproachfully. After the cough there is only silence with* IVANOV *intermittently striking his triangle, and the orchestra miming.*)

IVANOV: Better—good—much better . . .
  (ALEXANDER *is trying not to cough.*
  IVANOV *finishes with a final beat on the triangle.*
  The orchestra finishes.
  IVANOV *sits down.* ALEXANDER *coughs luxuriously.*)

IVANOV: (*Apologetically*) I know what you're thinking.

ALEXANDER: (*Understandingly*) It's all right.

IVANOV: No, you can say it. The cellos are rubbish.

ALEXANDER: (*Cautiously*) I'm not really a judge of music.

IVANOV: I was scraping the bottom of the barrel, and that's how they sound. And what about the horns?—should I persevere with them?

ALEXANDER: The horns?

IVANOV: Brazen to a man but mealy-mouthed. Butter wouldn't melt. When I try to reason with them they purse their lips. Tell me, do you have an opinion on the fungoid log-rollers spreading wet rot through the woodwinds? Not to speak of the glockenspiel.

ALEXANDER: The glockenspiel?

IVANOV: I asked you not to speak of it. Give me a word for the harpist.

16

ALEXANDER: I don't really—

IVANOV: Plucky. A harpist who rushes in where a fool would fear to tread—with all my problems you'd think I'd be spared exquisite irony. I've got a blue-arsed bassoon, a blue-tongued contra-bassoon, an organ grinder's chimpani, and the bass drum is in urgent need of a dermatologist.

ALEXANDER: Your condition is interesting.

IVANOV: I've got a violin section which is to violin playing what Heifetz is to water-polo. I've got a tubercular great-nephew of John Philip Sousa who goes oom when he should be going pah. And the Jew's harp has applied for a visa. I'm seriously thinking of getting a new orchestra. Do you read music?

ALEXANDER: No.

IVANOV: Don't worry: crochets, minims, sharp, flat, every good boy deserves favour. You'll pick it up in no time. What is your instrument?

ALEXANDER: I do not play an instrument.

IVANOV: Percussion? Strings? Brass?

ALEXANDER: No.

IVANOV: Reed? Keyboard?

ALEXANDER: I'm afraid not.

IVANOV: I'm amazed. Not keyboard. Wait a minute—flute.

ALEXANDER: No. Really.

IVANOV: Extraordinary. Give me a clue. If I beat you to a pulp would you try to protect your face or your hands? Which would be the more serious—if you couldn't sit down for a week or couldn't stand up? I'm trying to narrow it down, you see. Can I take it you don't stick this instrument up your arse in a kneeling position?

ALEXANDER: I do not play an instrument.

IVANOV: You can speak frankly. You will find I am without prejudice. I have invited musicians *into my own house*. And do you know why?—because we all have some musician in us. Any man says he has no musician in him, I'll call that man a *bigot*. Listen, I've had clarinet players eating *at my own table*. I've had French whores and gigolos speak to me in the *public street*, I mean horns, I mean piccolos, so don't worry about *me*, maestro, I've sat down with them, *drummers* even, sharing a plate of tagliatelle Verdi and stuffed Puccini

—why, I know people who make the orchestra eat in the kitchen, off scraps, the way you'd throw a trombone to a dog, I mean a second violinist, I mean to the lions; I love musicians, I respect them, human beings to a man. Let me put it like this: if I smashed this instrument of yours over your head, would you need a carpenter, a welder, or a brain surgeon?

ALEXANDER: I do not play an instrument. If I played an instrument I'd tell you what it was. But I do not play one. I have never played one. I do not know how to play one. I am not a musician.

IVANOV: What the hell are you doing here?

ALEXANDER: I was put here.

IVANOV: What for?

ALEXANDER: For slander.

IVANOV: Slander? What a fool! *Never speak ill of a musician!*— those bastards won't rest. They're animals, to a man.

ALEXANDER: This was political.

IVANOV: Let me give you some advice. Number one—never mix music with politics. Number two—never confide in your psychiatrist. Number three—*practise!*

ALEXANDER: Thank you.

(IVANOV *strikes his triangle once.*
The CELL *lighting fades.*
Percussion band. The music is that of a band of young children. It includes strings but they are only plucked.
Pretty soon the percussion performance goes wrong because there is a subversive triangle in it. The triangle is struck randomly and then rapidly, until finally it is the only instrument to be heard. And then the triangle stops.)

SCHOOL
The lights come up on the TEACHER *and* SACHA. *The* TEACHER *is holding a triangle.*

TEACHER: Well? Are you colour blind?

SACHA: No.

TEACHER: Let me see your music.

(SACHA *has sheet music on his desk.*)

Very well. What are the red notes?

SACHA: Strings.

18

TEACHER: Green?

SACHA: Tambourine.

TEACHER: Purple?

SACHA: Drum.

TEACHER: Yellow?

SACHA: Triangle.

TEACHER: Do you see forty yellow notes in a row?

SACHA: No.

TEACHER: What then? Detention is becoming a family tradition.
Your name is notorious. Did you know that?

SACHA: Yes.

TEACHER: How did you know?

SACHA: Everybody tells me.

TEACHER: Open a book.

SACHA: What book?

TEACHER: Any book. *Fathers and Sons*, perhaps.
(SACHA *takes a book out of the desk.*)
Is it Turgenev?

SACHA: It's my geometry book.

TEACHER: Yes, your name goes round the world. By telegram. It
is printed in the newspapers. It is spoken on the radio. With
such a famous name why should you bother with different
colours? We will change the music for you. It will look like
a field of buttercups, and sound like dinnertime.

SACHA: I don't want to be in the orchestra.

TEACHER: Open the book. Pencil and paper. You see what
happens to anti-social malcontents.

SACHA: Will I be sent to the lunatics' prison?

TEACHER: Certainly not. Read aloud.

SACHA: 'A point has position but no dimension.'

TEACHER: The asylum is for malcontents who don't know what
they're doing.

SACHA: 'A line has length but no breadth.'

TEACHER: They know what they're doing but they don't know
it's anti-social.

SACHA: 'A straight line is the shortest distance between two
points.'

TEACHER: They know it's anti-social but they're fanatics.

SACHA: 'A circle is the path of a point moving equidistant to a given point.'

TEACHER: They're sick.

SACHA: 'A polygon is a plane area bounded by straight lines.'

TEACHER: And it's not a prison, it's a hospital.

(*Pause.*)

SACHA: 'A triangle is the polygon bounded by the fewest possible sides.'

TEACHER: Good. Perfect. Copy neatly ten times, and if you're a good boy I might find you a better instrument.

SACHA: (*Writing*) 'A triangle is the polygon bounded by the fewest possible sides.' Is this what they make papa do?

TEACHER: Yes. They make him copy, 'I am a member of an orchestra and we must play together.'

SACHA: How many times?

TEACHER: A million.

SACHA: A million?

(*Pause.*)

(*Cries.*) Papa!

ALEXANDER: (*Cries*) Sacha!

(*This cry is* ALEXANDER *shouting in his sleep at the other end of the stage.*

IVANOV *sits watching* ALEXANDER.

The orchestra plays chords between the following.)

SACHA: Papa!

TEACHER: Hush!

ALEXANDER: Sacha!

(*The orchestra continues with percussion element for perhaps ten seconds and then is sabotaged by a triangle beaten rapidly, until the triangle is the only sound heard.*

ALEXANDER *sits up and the triangle stops.*)

CELL

IVANOV: Dinner time. (*Orchestra.*)

OFFICE

IVANOV *goes to sit at the table in the* OFFICE, *which is now the lit area.*

In the orchestra one of the lowliest violinists leaves his place. The orchestra accompanies and parodies this man's actions as he leaves the platform and enters the OFFICE. IVANOV *is sitting at the table on one of the chairs. The man* (DOCTOR) *puts his violin on the table. The orchestra has been following him the whole time and the* DOCTOR'*s movements fit precisely to the music.*

IVANOV *jumps up from his chair and shouts in the general direction of the orchestra.*

IVANOV: All right, all right!

> (*The music cuts out. The* DOCTOR *pauses looking at* IVANOV.)

IVANOV: (*To the* DOCTOR) I'm sorry about that.

> (IVANOV *sits down.*
> *The* DOCTOR *sits down and all the strings accompany this movement into his chair.*
> IVANOV *leaps up again.*)
> (*Shouts.*) I'll have your gut for garters!

DOCTOR: Sit down, please.

IVANOV: (*Sitting down*) It's the only kind of language they understand.

DOCTOR: Did the pills help at all?

IVANOV: I don't know. What pills did you give them?

DOCTOR: Now look, *there is no orchestra.* We cannot make progress until we agree that there is no orchestra.

IVANOV: Or until we agree that there is.

DOCTOR: (*Slapping his violin, which is on the table*) But there is no orchestra.

> (IVANOV *glances at the violin.*)
> I have an orchestra, but you do not.

IVANOV: Does that seem reasonable to you?

DOCTOR: It just happens to be so. I play in an orchestra occasionally. It is my hobby. It is a real orchestra. Yours is not. I am a doctor. You are a patient. If I tell you you do not have an orchestra, it follows that you do not have an orchestra. If you tell me you have an orchestra, it follows that you do not have an orchestra. Or rather it does not follow that you do have an orchestra.

IVANOV: I am perfectly happy not to have an orchestra.

DOCTOR: Good.

IVANOV: I never asked to have an orchestra.

DOCTOR: Keep saying to yourself, 'I have no orchestra. I have never had an orchestra. I do not want an orchestra.'

IVANOV: Absolutely.

DOCTOR: 'There is no orchestra.'

IVANOV: All right.

DOCTOR: Good.

IVANOV: There is one thing you can do for me.

DOCTOR: Yes?

IVANOV: Stop them playing.

DOCTOR: They will stop playing when you understand that they
do not exist.

(IVANOV *gets up*.)

IVANOV: I have no orchestra.

(*Music. 1 chord.*)

I have never had an orchestra.

(*Music. 2 chords.*)

I do not want an orchestra.

(*Music. 3 chords.*)

There is no orchestra.

(*The orchestra takes off in triumph.*

Light fades on OFFICE, *comes up on* CELL.)

CELL

ALEXANDER *has been asleep on his bed the whole time.* IVANOV *returns
to the* CELL. *He picks up his triangle rod. He stands by* ALEXANDER's
*bed looking down on him. The music continues and becomes threaten-
ing. It becomes nightmare music.* ALEXANDER's *nightmare. The music
seems to be approaching violent catharsis. But* ALEXANDER *jumps
awake and the music cuts out in mid-bar.*

Silence.

IVANOV: Sorry. I can't control them.

ALEXANDER: Please . . .

IVANOV: Don't worry, I know how to handle myself. Any
trumpeter comes at me, I'll kick his teeth in. Violins get it
under the chin to boot, this boot, and God help anyone
who plays a cello. Do you play a musical instrument?

ALEXANDER: No.

IVANOV: Then you've got nothing to worry about. Tell me about
yourself—your home, your childhood, your first piano-
teacher . . . how did it all begin?

(*The next speech should be lit as a sort of solo. Musical annotation.*)

ALEXANDER: One day they arrested a friend of mine for possessing a controversial book, and they kept him in mental hospitals for a year and a half. I thought this was an odd thing to do. Soon after he got out, they arrested a couple of writers, A and B, who had published some stories abroad under different names. Under their own names they got five years' and seven years' hard labour. I thought this was most peculiar. My friend, C, demonstrated against the arrest of A and B. I told him he was crazy to do it, and they put him back into the mental hospital. D was a man who wrote to various people about the trial of A and B and held meetings with his friends E, F, G and H, who were all arrested, so I, J, K, L and a fifth man demonstrated against the arrest of E, F, G and H, and were themselves arrested. D was arrested the next day. The fifth man was my friend C, who had just got out of the mental hospital where they put him for demonstrating against the arrest of A and B, and I told him he was crazy to demonstrate against the arrest of E, F, G and H, and he got three years in a labour camp. I thought this really wasn't fair. M compiled a book on the trials of C, I, J, K and L, and with his colleagues N, O, P, Q, R and S attended the trial of T who had written a book about his experiences in a labour camp, and who got a year in a labour camp. In the courtroom it was learned that the Russian army had gone to the aid of Czechoslovakia. M, N, O, P, Q, R and S decided to demonstrate in Red Square the following Sunday, when they were all arrested and variously disposed of in labour camps, psychiatric hospitals and internal exile. Three years had passed since the arrest of A and B. C finished his sentence about the same time as A, and then he did something really crazy. He started telling everybody that sane people were being put in mental hospitals for their political opinions. By the time B finished his sentence, C was on trial for anti-Soviet agitation and slander, and he got seven years in prison and labour camps, and five years' exile.

You see all the trouble writers cause.

(*The children's percussion band re-enters as a discreet subtext.*)

They spoil things for ordinary people.

My childhood was uneventful. My adolescence was normal. I got an ordinary job, and married a conventional girl who died uncontroversially in childbirth. Until the child was seven the only faintly interesting thing about me was that I had a friend who kept getting arrested.

Then one day I did something really crazy.

(*The percussion is sabotaged exactly as before but this time by a snare drum being violently beaten. It stops suddenly and the light comes up on* SACHA *sitting at the desk with a punctured drum on the desk, the* TEACHER *standing motionless in her position. Optional: On tape the sound of a children's playground at some distance.*)

SCHOOL

TEACHER: So this is how I am repaid. Is this how it began with your father? First he smashes school property. Later he keeps bad company. Finally, slanderous letters. Lies. To his superiors. To the Party. To the newspapers. . . . To foreigners. . . .

SACHA: Papa doesn't lie. He beat me when I did it.

TEACHER: *Lies!* Bombarding *Pravda* with lies! What did he expect?

(*The light on the* TEACHER *and* SACHA *fades just after the beginning of* ALEXANDER'*s speech.*)

CELL

ALEXANDER: They put me in the Leningrad Special Psychiatric Hospital on Arsenal'naya Street, where I was kept for thirty months, including two months on hunger strike.

They don't like you to die unless you can die anonymously. If your name is known in the West, it is an embarrassment. The bad old days were over long ago. Things are different now. Russia is a civilized country, very good at Swan Lake and space technology, and it is confusing if people starve themselves to death.

So after a couple of weeks they brought my son to persuade me to eat. But although by this time he was nine years old he was uncertain what to say.

(SACHA *speaks from the* SCHOOL, *not directly to* ALEXANDER.)

24

SACHA: I got a letter from abroad, with our picture in the newspaper.

ALEXANDER: What did it say?

SACHA: I don't know. It was all in English.

ALEXANDER: How is school?

SACHA: All right. I've started geometry. It's horrible.

ALEXANDER: How is Babushka?

SACHA: All right. You smell like Olga when she does her nails.

ALEXANDER: Who is Olga?

SACHA: She has your room now. Till you come back.

ALEXANDER: Good.

SACHA: Do they make you paint your nails here?

(End of duologue. Return to solo.)

ALEXANDER: If you don't eat for a long time you start to smell of acetone, which is the stuff girls use for taking the paint off their finger-nails. When the body runs out of protein and carbohydrate it starts to metabolize its own fat, and acetone is the waste product. To put this another way, a girl removing her nail-varnish smells of starvation.

After two months you could have removed nail-varnish with my urine, so they brought Sacha back, but when he saw me he couldn't speak—

SACHA: *(Cries)* Papa!

ALEXANDER: —and then they gave in. And when I was well enough they brought me here.

This means they have decided to let me go. It is much harder to get from Arsenal'naya to a civil hospital than from a civil hospital to the street. But it has to be done right. They don't want to lose ground. They need a formula. It will take a little time but that's all right. I shall read *War and Peace*.

Everything is going to be all right.

(Orchestra.)

SCHOOL

This scene is enclosed inside music which ends up as the DOCTOR's *violin solo into the following scene.*

SACHA: A triangle is the shortest distance between three points.

TEACHER: Rubbish.

SACHA: A circle is the longest distance to the same point.

TEACHER: Sacha!

SACHA: A plane area bordered by high walls is a prison not a
hospital.

TEACHER: Be quiet!

SACHA: I don't care!—he was never sick at home. Never!
(*Music.*)

TEACHER: Stop crying.
(*Music.*)
Everything is going to be all right.
(*Music to violin solo.*
Lights fade on SCHOOL.)

OFFICE

DOCTOR *in his* OFFICE *playing violin solo. Violin cuts out.*

DOCTOR: Come in.
(ALEXANDER *enters the* DOCTOR'*s light.*)

DOCTOR: Hello. Sit down please. Do you play a musical
instrument?

ALEXANDER: (*Taken aback*) Are you a patient?

DOCTOR: (*Cheerfully*) No, I am a doctor. *You* are a patient. It's a
distinction which we try to keep going here, though I'm
told it's coming under scrutiny in more advanced circles of
psychiatric medicine. (*He carefully puts his violin into its case.*)
(*Sententiously*) Yes, if everybody in the world played a
violin, I'd be out of a job.

ALEXANDER: As a psychiatrist?

DOCTOR: No, as a violinist. The psychiatric hospitals would be
packed to the doors. You obviously don't know much about
musicians. Welcome to the Third Civil Mental Hospital.
What can I do for you?

ALEXANDER: I have a complaint.

DOCTOR: (*Opening file*) Yes, I know—pathological development of
the personality with paranoid delusions.

ALEXANDER: No, there's nothing the matter with me.

DOCTOR: (*Closing file*) There you are, you see.

ALEXANDER: My complaint is about the man in my cell.

DOCTOR: Ward.

ALEXANDER: He thinks he has an orchestra.

26

DOCTOR: Yes, he has an identity problem. I forget his name.

ALEXANDER: His behaviour is aggressive.

DOCTOR: He complains about you, too. Apparently you cough during the diminuendos.

ALEXANDER: Is there anything you can do?

DOCTOR: Certainly. (*Producing a red pill box from the drawer.*) Suck one of these every four hours.

ALEXANDER: But he's a raving lunatic.

DOCTOR: Of course. The idea that all the people locked up in mental hospitals are sane while the people walking about outside are all mad is merely a literary conceit, put about by people who should be locked up. I assure you there's not much in it. Taken as a whole, the sane are out there and the sick are in here. For example, *you* are here because you have delusions, that sane people are put in mental hospitals.

ALEXANDER: But I *am* in a mental hospital.

DOCTOR: That's what I said. If you're not prepared to discuss your case rationally, we're going to go round in circles. Did you say you *didn't* play a musical instrument, by the way?

ALEXANDER: No. Could I be put in a cell on my own?

DOCTOR: Look, let's get this clear. This is what is called an *Ordinary* Psychiatric Hospital, that is to say a civil mental hospital coming under the Ministry of Heath, and we have *wards*. Cells is what they have in prisons, and also, possibly, in what are called *Special* Psychiatric Hospitals, which come under the Ministry of Internal Affairs and are for prisoners who represent a special danger to society. Or rather, patients. No, you didn't say, or no you don't play one?

ALEXANDER: Could I be put in a ward on my own?

DOCTOR: I'm afraid not. Colonel—or rather Doctor—Rozinsky, who has taken over your case, chose your cell- or rather ward-mate personally.

ALEXANDER: He might kill me.

DOCTOR: We have to assume that Rozinsky knows what's best for you; though in my opinion you need a psychiatrist.

ALEXANDER: You mean he's not really a doctor?

DOCTOR: Of course he's a doctor and he is proud to serve the State in any capacity, but he was not actually trained in psychiatry *as such*.

27

ALEXANDER: What is his speciality?

DOCTOR: Semantics. He's a Doctor of Philology, whatever that means. I'm told he's a genius.

ALEXANDER: (*Angrily*) I won't see him.

DOCTOR: It may not be necessary. It seems to me that the best answer is for you to go home. Would Thursday suit you?

ALEXANDER: Thursday?

DOCTOR: Why not? There is an Examining Commission on Wednesday. We shall aim at curing your schizophrenia by Tuesday night, if possible by seven o'clock because I have a concert. (*He produces a large blue pill box.*) Take one of these every four hours.

ALEXANDER: What are they?

DOCTOR: A mild laxative.

ALEXANDER: For schizophrenia?

DOCTOR: The layman often doesn't realize that medicine advances in a series of imaginative leaps.

ALEXANDER: I see. Well, I suppose I'll have to read *War and Peace* some other time.

DOCTOR: Yes. Incidentally, when you go before the Commission try not to make any remark which might confuse them. I shouldn't mention *War and Peace* unless they mention it first. The sort of thing I'd stick to is 'Yes', if they ask you whether you agree you were mad; 'No', if they ask you whether you intend to persist in your slanders; 'Definitely', if they ask you whether your treatment has been satisfactory, and 'Sorry', if they ask you how you feel about it all, or if you didn't catch the question.

ALEXANDER: I was never mad, and my treatment was barbaric.

DOCTOR: Stupidity is one thing I can't cure. I have to show that I have treated you. You have to recant and show gratitude for the treatment. We have to act together.

ALEXANDER: The KGB broke my door and frightened my son and my mother-in-law. My madness consisted of writing to various people about a friend of mine who is in prison. This friend was twice put in mental hospitals for political reasons, and then they arrested him for saying that sane people were put in mental hospitals, and then they put him in prison because he was sane when he said this; and I said so, and

they put me in a mental hospital. And you are quite right—
in the Arsenal'naya they have cells. There are bars on the
windows, peepholes in the doors, and the lights burn all
night. It is run just like a gaol, with warders and trusties,
but the regime is more strict, and the male nurses are
convicted criminals serving terms for theft and violent
crimes, and they beat and humiliate the patients and steal
their food, and are protected by the doctors, some of whom
wear KGB uniforms under their white coats. For the
politicals, punishment and medical treatment are intimately
related. I was given injections of aminazin, sulfazin, triftazin,
haloperidol and insulin, which caused swellings, cramps,
headaches, trembling, fever and the loss of various abilities
including the ability to read, write, sleep, sit, stand, and
button my trousers. When all this failed to improve my
condition, I was stripped and bound head to foot with
lengths of wet canvas. As the canvas dried it became tighter
and tighter until I lost consciousness. They did this to me
for ten days in a row, and still my condition did not
improve.

Then I went on hunger strike. And when they saw I
intended to die they lost their nerve. And now you think
I'm going to crawl out of here, thanking them for curing
me of my delusions? Oh no. They lost. And they will have
to see that it is so. They have forgotten their mortality.
Losing might be their first touch of it for a long time.

(DOCTOR *picks up his violin.*)

DOCTOR: What about your son? He is turning into a delinquent.

(DOCTOR *plucks the violin EGBDF.*)

He's a good boy. He deserves a father.

(DOCTOR *plucks the violin . . .*)

SCHOOL

TEACHER: Things have changed since the bad old days. When I
was a girl there were terrible excesses. A man accused like
your father might well have been blameless. Now things are
different. The Constitution guarantees freedom of conscience,
freedom of the press, freedom of speech, of assembly, of
worship, and many other freedoms. The Soviet Constitution

29

has always been the most liberal in the world, ever since the first Constitution was written after the Revolution.

SACHA: Who wrote it?

TEACHER: (*Hesitates*) His name was Nikolai Bukharin.

SACHA: Can we ask Nikolai Bukharin about papa?

TEACHER: Unfortunately he was shot soon after he wrote the Constitution. Everything was different in those days. Terrible things happened.

CELL

ALEXANDER *has just started to read 'War and Peace' and* IVANOV *looks over his shoulder.*

IVANOV: 'Well, prince, Genoa and Lucca are no more than the private estates of the Bonaparte family.'

(ALEXANDER *is nervous, and* IVANOV *becomes hysterical but still reading.*)

'If you dare deny that this means war—'

(ALEXANDER *jumps up slamming the book shut and the orchestra jumps into a few bars of the '1812'.* IVANOV *holds* ALEXANDER *by the shoulders and there is a moment of suspense and imminent violence, then* IVANOV *kisses* ALEXANDER *on both cheeks.*)

Courage, mon brave!

Every member of the orchestra carries a baton in his knapsack! Your turn will come.

OFFICE

DOCTOR: Next!

(ALEXANDER *goes into the* OFFICE.)

Your behaviour is causing alarm. I'm beginning to think you're off your head. Quite apart from being a paranoid schizophrenic. I have to consider seriously whether an Ordinary Hospital can deal with your symptoms.

ALEXANDER: I have no symptoms, I have opinions.

DOCTOR: Your opinions are your symptoms. Your disease is dissent. Your kind of schizophrenia does not presuppose changes of personality noticeable to others. I might compare your case to that of Pyotr Grigorenko of whom it has been stated by our leading psychiatrists at the Serbsky Institute, that his outwardly well adjusted behaviour and formally coherent utterances were indicative of a pathological development of the personality. Are you getting the message? I can't help you. And furthermore your breath stinks of aeroplane glue or something—what have you been eating?

ALEXANDER: Nothing.

DOCTOR: And that's something else—we have never had a hunger strike here, except once and that was in protest against the food, which is psychologically coherent and it did wonders for the patients' morale, though not for the food. . . .
(*Pause.*)
You can choose your own drugs.
You don't even have to take them.
Just say you took them.
(*Pause.*)
Well, what do you *want*?

ALEXANDER: (*Flatly, not poetically*)
I want to get back to the bad old times
when a man got a sentence appropriate to his crimes—
ten years' hard for a word out of place,
twenty-five years if they didn't like your face,
and no one pretended that you were off your head.
In the good old Archipelago you're either well or dead—
And the—

DOCTOR: Stop it!
My God, how long can you go on like that?

ALEXANDER: In the Arsenal'naya I was not allowed writing materials, on medical grounds. If you want to remember things it helps if they rhyme.

DOCTOR: You gave me a dreadful shock. I thought I had discovered an entirely new form of mental disturbance. Immortality smiled upon me, one quick smile, and was gone.

ALEXANDER: Your name may not be entirely lost to history.

DOCTOR: What do you mean?—it's not *me*! I'm told what to do. Look, if you'll eat something I'll send for your son.

ALEXANDER: I don't want him to come here.

DOCTOR: If you don't eat something I'll send for your son.
(*Pause.*)

You mustn't be so rigid.

(ALEXANDER *starts to leave.*

Pause.)

Did the pills help at all?

ALEXANDER: I don't know.

DOCTOR: Do you believe that sane people are put in mental hospitals?

ALEXANDER: Yes.

DOCTOR: They didn't help.

ALEXANDER: I gave them to Ivanov. *His* name is also Ivanov.

DOCTOR: So it is. That's why Colonel or rather Doctor Rozinsky insisted you shared his cell, or rather ward.

ALEXANDER: Because we have the same name?

DOCTOR: The man is a genius. The layman often doesn't realize that medicine advances in—

ALEXANDER: I know. I have been giving Ivanov my rations. He needed a laxative. I gave him my pills.

(ALEXANDER *leaves.*)

DOCTOR: Next!

(IVANOV *enters immediately, with his triangle, almost crossing* ALEXANDER.

IVANOV *is transformed, triumphant, awe-struck.*)

Hello, Ivanov. Did the pills help at all?

(IVANOV *strikes his triangle.*)

IVANOV: I have no orchestra!

(*Silence.*)

IVANOV *indicates the silence with a raised finger. He strikes his triangle again.*)

DOCTOR: (*Suddenly*) Wait a minute!—what day is it?

IVANOV: I have never *had* an orchestra!

(*Silence.*

The DOCTOR, *however, has become preoccupied and misses the significance of this.*)

DOCTOR: *What day is it?* Tuesday?

(IVANOV *strikes the triangle.*)

IVANOV: I do not want an orchestra!

(*Silence.*)

DOCTOR: (*Horrified*) What time is it? I'm going to be late for the orchestra!

(*The* DOCTOR *grabs his violin case and starts to leave.* IVANOV *strikes his triangle.*)

IVANOV: *There is no orchestra!*

DOCTOR: (*Leaving*) Of course there's a bloody orchestra!

(*Music—one chord.* IVANOV *hears it and is mortified. More chords. The* DOCTOR *has left.*)

IVANOV: (*Bewildered*) I have an orchestra.

(*Music.*)

I've *always* had an orchestra.

(*Music.*)

I always *knew* I had an orchestra.

(*Music.*

ALEXANDER *has gone to sit on his bed.* IVANOV *sits in the* DOCTOR's *chair. The* DOCTOR *joins the violinists.* SACHA *moves across towards* IVANOV.

The music continues and ends.)

IVANOV: Come in.

SACHA: Alexander Ivanov, sir.

IVANOV: Absolutely correct. Who are you?

SACHA: Alexander Ivanov, sir.

IVANOV: The boy's a fool.

SACHA: They said to come, sir. Is it about my father?

IVANOV: What's his name?

SACHA: Alexander Ivanov, sir.

IVANOV: This place is a madhouse.

SACHA: I know, sir.

Are you the doctor?

IVANOV: *Ivanov!* Of course. Sad case.

SACHA: What's the matter with him?

IVANOV: Tone deaf. Are you musical at all?

SACHA: No, sir.

IVANOV: What is your instrument?

SACHA: Triangle, sir.

Is it about *that* that I'm here?

IVANOV: Certainly, what else?

SACHA: Drum, sir.

IVANOV: What?

SACHA: Don't make me stay! I'll go back in the orchestra!

IVANOV: You can be in mine.

33

SACHA: I can't play anything, really.

IVANOV: Everyone is equal to the triangle. That is the first axiom
of Euclid, the Greek musician.

SACHA: Yes, sir.

IVANOV: The second axiom! It is easier for a sick man to play
the triangle than for a camel to play the triangle.

The third axiom!—even a camel can play the triangle!

The *pons asinorum* of Euclid! Anyone can play the triangle
no matter how sick!

SACHA: Yes, sir—(*Crying.*)—please will you put me with Papa?

IVANOV (*Raving*) The five postulates of Euclid!

A triangle with a bass is a combo!

Two triangles sharing the same bass is a trio!

SACHA: Are you the doctor?

IVANOV: A trombone is the longest distance between two points!

SACHA: You're not the doctor.

IVANOV: A string has length but no point.

SACHA: (*Cries*) Papa!

IVANOV: What is the Golden Rule?

SACHA: Papa!

IVANOV: (*Shouts*) A line *must be drawn*!

SACHA *runs out of* IVANOV's *light and moves into the orchestra among
the players. The next four of* SACHA's *speeches, which are sung, come
from different positions as he moves around the orchestra platform.
There is music involved in the following scene.*

SACHA: (*Sings*) Papa, where've they put you?

(ALEXANDER's '*poems*' *are uttered rapidly on a single rhythm.*)

ALEXANDER: Dear Sacha, don't be sad,
          it would have been ten times as bad
          if we hadn't had the time we had,
          so think of that and please be glad.
          I kiss you now, your loving dad.
          Don't let them tell you I was mad.

SACHA: (*Sings*) Papa, don't be rigid!

Everything can be all right!

ALEXANDER: Dear Sacha, try to see
          what they call their liberty
          is just the freedom to agree

34

that one and one is sometimes three.
I kiss you now, remember me.
Don't neglect your geometry.

SACHA: (*Sings*) Papa, don't be rigid!
Everything can be all right!

ALEXANDER: Dear Sacha, when I'd dead,
I'll be living in your head,
which is what your mama said,
keep her picture by your bed.
I kiss you now, and don't forget,
if you're brave the best is yet.

SACHA: (*Sings*) Papa, don't be rigid!
Be brave and tell them lies!

CELL

SACHA: (*Not singing*) Tell them lies. Tell them they've cured you.
Tell them you're grateful.

ALEXANDER: How can that be right?

SACHA: If they're wicked how can it be wrong?

ALEXANDER: It helps them to go on being wicked. It helps people
to think that perhaps they're not so wicked after all.

SACHA: It doesn't matter. I want you to come home.

ALEXANDER: And what about all the other fathers? And mothers?

SACHA: (*Shouts*) It's wicked to let yourself die!
(SACHA *leaves*.)

The DOCTOR *moves from the orchestra to the* SCHOOL.

DOCTOR: Ivanov!

ALEXANDER: Dear Sacha—
be glad of—
kiss Mama's picture—
good-bye.

DOCTOR: Ivanov!
(IVANOV *moves to* CELL.)
Ivanov!
(SACHA *moves towards the* SCHOOL.)

ALEXANDER: (*Rapidly as before*)
Dear Sacha, I love you,
I hope you love me too.

To thine own self be true
one and one is always two.
I kiss you now, adieu.
There was nothing else to do.

SCHOOL

SACHA *arrives at* SCHOOL. DOCTOR *is there.*

TEACHER *has remained near the desk.*

TEACHER: Sacha. Did you persuade him?

SACHA: He's going to die.

DOCTOR: I'm not allowed to let him die.

SACHA: Then let him go.

DOCTOR: I'm not allowed to let him go till he admits he's cured.

SACHA: Then he'll die.

DOCTOR: He'd rather die than admit he's cured? This is madness, and it's not allowed!

SACHA: Then you'll have to let him go.

DOCTOR: I'm not allowed to—it's a logical impasse. Did you tell him he mustn't be so rigid?

SACHA: If you want to get rid of Papa, *you* must not be rigid!

DOCTOR: What shall I tell the Colonel? He's a genius but he can't do the impossible.

(*Organ music. The* COLONEL'*s entrance is as impressive as possible. The organ accompanies his entrance.*

The DOCTOR *moves to meet him. The* COLONEL *ignores the* DOCTOR. *He stops in front of* ALEXANDER *and* IVANOV. *When the organ music stops the* COLONEL *speaks.*)

CELL

COLONEL: Ivanov!

(ALEXANDER *and* IVANOV *stand up.*)

(*To* IVANOV.) Alexander Ivanov?

IVANOV: Yes.

COLONEL: Do you believe that sane people are put in mental hospitals?

DOCTOR: Excuse me, Doctor—

COLONEL: Shut up!—

(*To* IVANOV.) Well? Would a Soviet doctor put a sane man into a lunatic asylum, in your opinion?

36

IVANOV: (*Baffled*) I shouldn't think so. Why?

COLONEL: (*Briskly*) Quite right! How do you feel?

IVANOV: Fit as a fiddle, thank you.

COLONEL: Quite right!

(*The* COLONEL *turns to* ALEXANDER.)

Alexander Ivanov?

ALEXANDER: Yes.

COLONEL: Do you have an orchestra?

(IVANOV *opens his mouth to speak.*)

(*To* IVANOV.) Shut up!

(*To* ALEXANDER.) Well?

ALEXANDER: No.

COLONEL: Do you hear any music of any kind?

ALEXANDER: No.

COLONEL: How do you feel?

ALEXANDER: All right.

COLONEL: Manners!

ALEXANDER: Thank you.

COLONEL: (*To* DOCTOR) There's absolutely nothing wrong with these men. Get them out of here.

DOCTOR: Yes, Colonel—Doctor.

(*The* COLONEL'*s exit is almost as impressive as his entrance, also with organ music. But this time the organ music blends into orchestral music—the finale.*)

The TEACHER *moves into the orchestra. The* DOCTOR *moves to the violins taking his instrument and joining in.* IVANOV *takes his triangle and joins the percussionists and beats the triangle.*

SACHA *comes across to the middle of the platform at the bottom. These directions assume a centre aisle going up the middle of the orchestra towards the organ.* ALEXANDER *and* SACHA *move up this aisle,* SACHA *running ahead. At the top he turns and sings to the same tune as before:*

SACHA: (*Sings*) Papa, don't be crazy!

Everything can be all right!

ALEXANDER: Sacha—

SACHA: (*Sings*) Everything can be all right!

(*Music. Music ends.*)

PROFESSIONAL FOUL
A Play for Television

To Vaclav Havel

Characters

ANDERSON
MCKENDRICK
CHETWYN
HOLLAR
BROADBENT
CRISP
STONE
CAPTAIN (MAN 6)
POLICEMAN (MAN 1)
POLICEMAN (MAN 2)
POLICEMAN (MAN 3)
POLICEMAN (MAN 4)
POLICEMAN (MAN 5)
MRS HOLLAR
SACHA (ten years old)
GRAYSON
CHAMBERLAIN
FRENCHMAN
CHAIRMAN
CLERK, LIFT OPERATORS, CONCIERGES,
INTERPRETERS, CUSTOMS, POLICE, etc.

Professional Foul was first shown on BBC TV in September 1977. The cast was as follows:

ANDERSON	Peter Barkworth
MCKENDRICK	John Shrapnel
CHETWYN	Richard O'Callaghan
HOLLAR	Stephen Rea
BROADBENT	Bernard Hill
CRISP	Billy Hamon
STONE	Shane Rimmer
CAPTAIN	David de Keyser
MAN 1	Ludwig Lang
MAN 2	Milos Kirek
MAN 3	Arnoft Kopecky
MAN 4	Paul Moritz
MRS HOLLAR	Susan Strawson
SACHA	Stefan Ceba
GRAYSON	Sam Kelly
CHAMBERLAIN	Victor Longley
FRENCHMAN	Graeme Eton
CHAIRMAN	Ivan Jelinek
CLERK	Patrick Monckton
INTERPRETER	Sandra Frieze
Script Editor	Richard Broke
Designer	Don Taylor
Producer	Mark Shivas
Director	Michael Lindsay-Hogg

1. INT. AEROPLANE. IN FLIGHT

The tourist class cabin of a passenger jet.

We are mainly concerned with two passengers. ANDERSON *is an Ox-bridge don, a professor. He is middle-aged, or more. He is sitting in an aisle seat, on the left as we look down the gangway towards the tail.* MCKENDRICK *is also in an aisle seat, but across the gangway and one row nearer the tail.* MCKENDRICK *is about forty. He is also a don, but where* ANDERSON *gives a somewhat fastidious impression,* MCKENDRICK *is a rougher sort of diamond.*

MCKENDRICK *is sitting in the first row of smokers' seats, and* ANDERSON *in the last row of the non-smokers' seats looking aft.*

The plane is by no means full. The three seats across the aisle from ANDERSON *are vacant. The seat next to* ANDERSON *on his right is also vacant but the seat beyond that, by the window, accommodates a* SLEEPING MAN.

On the vacant seat between ANDERSON *and the* SLEEPING MAN *is lying a sex magazine of the* Penthouse *type. The magazine, however, is as yet face down.*

The passengers are coming to the end of a meal. They have trays of aeroplane food in front of them.

MCKENDRICK *puts down his fork and lights a cigarette.*

ANDERSON *dabs at his mouth with his napkin and puts it down. He glances around casually and notes the magazine next to him. He notes the* SLEEPING MAN.

MCKENDRICK *has a briefcase on the seat next to him, and from this he takes a glossy brochure. In fact, this is quite an elaborate publication associated with a philosophical congress. The cover of this programme is seen to read: 'Colloquium Philosophicum Prague 77'.*

ANDERSON *slides out from under his lunch tray a brochure identical to* MCKENDRICK'S. *He glances at it for a mere moment and loses interest. He turns his attention back to the magazine on the seat. He turns the*

43

magazine over and notes the naked woman on its cover. He picks the magazine up, with a further glance at the SLEEPING MAN, *and opens it to a spread of colour photographs. Consciously or unconsciously he is holding the brochure in such a way as to provide a shield for the magazine.*

MCKENDRICK *casually glancing round, sees the twin to his own brochure.*

MCKENDRICK: Snap.

> (ANDERSON *looks up guiltily.*)

ANDERSON: Ah . . .

> (ANDERSON *closes the magazine and slides it face-up under his lunch tray.*
>
> MCKENDRICK'*s manner is extrovert. Almost breezy.*
>
> ANDERSON'*s manner is a little vague.*)

MCKENDRICK: I wasn't sure it was you. Not a very good likeness.

ANDERSON: I assure you this is how I look.

MCKENDRICK: I mean your photograph. (*He flips his brochure open. It contains small photographs and pen portraits of various men and women who are in fact to be speakers at the colloquium.*) The photograph is younger.

ANDERSON: It must be an old photograph.

> (MCKENDRICK *gets up and comes to sit in the empty seat across the aisle from* ANDERSON.)

MCKENDRICK: (*Changing seats*) Bill McKendrick.

ANDERSON: How odd.

MCKENDRICK: Is it?

ANDERSON: Young therefore old. Old therefore young. Only odd at first glance.

MCKENDRICK: Oh yes.

> (ANDERSON *takes a notebook, with pencil attached, from his pocket and writes in it as he speaks.*)

ANDERSON: The second glance is known as linguistic analysis. A lot of chaps pointing out that we don't always mean what we say, even when we manage to say what we mean. Personally I'm quite prepared to believe it. (*He finishes writing and closes the notebook. He glances uneasily out of the window.*) Have you noticed the way the wings keep *wagging*? I try to look away and think of something else but I am

drawn back irresistibly . . . I wouldn't be nervous about
flying if the wings didn't wag. Solid steel. Thick as a bank
safe. Flexing like tree branches. It's not natural. There is a
coldness around my heart as though I'd seen your
cigarette smoke knock against the ceiling and break in two
like a bread stick. By the way, that is a non-smoking seat.

MCKENDRICK: Sorry

(MCKENDRICK *stubs out his cigarette.* ANDERSON *puts his notebook
back into his pocket.*)

ANDERSON: Yes, I like to collect little curiosities for the language
chaps. It's like handing round a bag of liquorice allsorts.
They're terribly grateful. (*A thought strikes him.*) Oh, you're
not a language chap yourself?

(*The question seems to surprise* MCKENDRICK, *and amuse him.*)

MCKENDRICK: No. I'm McKendrick.

ANDERSON: You'll be giving a paper?

MCKENDRICK: Yes. Nothing new, actually. More of a summing-up
of my corner. My usual thing, you know . . . ?

(MCKENDRICK *is fishing but* ANDERSON *doesn't seem to notice.*)

ANDERSON: Jolly good.

MCKENDRICK: Perhaps you've come across some of my stuff . . . ?

(ANDERSON *now wakes up to the situation and is contrite.*)

ANDERSON: Clearly that is a reasonable expectation. I *am* sorry.
I'm sure I know your name. I don't read the philosophical
journals as much as I should, and hardly ever go to these
international bunfights. No time nowadays. They shouldn't
call us professors. It's more like being the faculty almoner.

MCKENDRICK: At least my paper will be new to you. We are the
only English, actually singing for our supper, I mean. I
expect there'll be a few others going for the free trip and
the social life. In fact, I see we've got one on board. At the
back.

(MCKENDRICK *jerks his head towards the back of the plane.*
ANDERSON *turns round to look. The object of attention is*
CHETWYN, *asleep in the back row, on the aisle.* CHETWYN *is
younger than* MCKENDRICK *and altogether frailer and neater.*
ANDERSON *squints down the plane at* CHETWYN.)

Do you know Prague?

ANDERSON: (*Warily*) Not personally. I know the name. (*Then he wakes up to that.*) Oh, *Prague.* Sorry. No, I've never been there. (*Small pause.*) Or have I? I got an honorary degree at Bratislava once. We changed planes in Prague. (*Pause.*) It might have been Vienna actually. (*Pause. He looks at the window.*) Wag, wag.

MCKENDRICK: It's Andrew Chetwyn. Do you know him?

ANDERSON: (*Warily*) Not personally.

MCKENDRICK: I don't know him *personally.* Do you know his line at all?

ANDERSON: Not as such.

MCKENDRICK: (*Suspiciously*) Have you *heard* of him?

ANDERSON: No. In a word.

MCKENDRICK: Oh. He's been quite public recently.

ANDERSON: He's an ethics chap is he?

MCKENDRICK: His line is that Aristotle got it more or less right, and St Augustine brought it up to date.

ANDERSON: I can see that that might make him conspicuous.

MCKENDRICK: Oh, it's not *that.* I mean politics. Letters to *The Times* about persecuted professors with unpronounceable names. I'm surprised the Czechs gave him a visa.

ANDERSON: There are some rather dubious things happening in Czechoslovakia. Ethically.

MCKENDRICK: Oh yes. No doubt.

ANDERSON: We must not try to pretend otherwise.

MCKENDRICK: Oh quite. I mean I don't. My work is pretty political. I mean by implication, of course. As yours is. I'm looking forward to hearing you.

ANDERSON: Thank you. I'm sure your paper will be very interesting too.

MCKENDRICK: As a matter of fact I think there's a lot of juice left in the fictions problem.

ANDERSON: Is that what you're speaking on?

MCKENDRICK: No—you are.

ANDERSON: Oh, am I? (*He looks in his brochure briefly.*) So I am.

MCKENDRICK: 'Ethical Fictions as Ethical Foundations'.

ANDERSON: Yes. To tell you the truth I have an ulterior motive for coming to Czechoslovakia at this time. I'm being a tiny bit naughty.

MCKENDRICK: Naughty?

ANDERSON: Unethical. Well, I am being paid for by the Czech government, after all.

MCKENDRICK: And what . . . ?

ANDERSON: I don't think I'm going to tell you. You see, if I tell you I make you a co-conspirator whether or not you would have wished to be one. Ethically I should give you the opportunity of choosing to be one or not.

MCKENDRICK: Then why don't you give me the opportunity?

ANDERSON: I can't without telling you. An impasse.

(MCKENDRICK *is already putting two and two together and cannot hide his curiosity.*)

MCKENDRICK: Look . . . Professor Anderson . . . if it's political in any way I'd really be very interested.

ANDERSON: Why, are you a politics chap?

MCKENDRICK: One is naturally interested in what is happening in these places. And I have an academic interest—my field is the philosophical assumptions of social science.

ANDERSON: How fascinating. What is that exactly?

MCKENDRICK: (*Slightly hurt*) Perhaps my paper tomorrow afternoon will give you a fair idea.

ANDERSON: (*Mortified*) Tomorrow afternoon? I say, what rotten luck. That's exactly when I have to play truant. I *am* sorry.

MCKENDRICK: (*Coldly*) That's all right.

ANDERSON: I expect they'll have copies.

MCKENDRICK: I expect so.

ANDERSON: The science of social philosophy, eh?

MCKENDRICK: (*Brusquely*) More or less.

ANDERSON: (*With polite interest*) McCarthy.

MCKENDRICK: McKendrick.

ANDERSON: And how are things at . . . er . . .

MCKENDRICK: Stoke.

ANDERSON: (*Enthusiastically*) Stoke! An excellent university, I believe.

MCKENDRICK: You know perfectly well you wouldn't be seen dead in it.

(ANDERSON *considers this.*)

ANDERSON: Even if that were true, my being seen dead in a place has never so far as I know been thought a condition of its excellence.

(MCKENDRICK *despite himself laughs, though somewhat bitterly.*)

MCKENDRICK: Very good.

(*An* AIR HOSTESS *is walking down the aisle removing people's lunch trays. She removes* ANDERSON's *tray, revealing the cover of the sexy magazine, in the middle of* MCKENDRICK's *next speech and passes down the aisle.*)

Wit and paradox. Verbal felicity. An occupation for gentlemen. A higher civilization alive and well in the older universities. I see you like tits and bums, by the way.

ANDERSON: (*Embarrassed*) Ah . . .

(*The turning of tables cheers* MCKENDRICK *up considerably.*)

MCKENDRICK: They won't let you in with that you know. You'll have to hide it.

ANDERSON: As a matter of fact it doesn't belong to me.

MCKENDRICK: Western decadence you see. Marxists are a terrible lot of prudes. I can say that because I'm a bit that way myself.

ANDERSON: You surprise me.

MCKENDRICK: Mind you, when I say I'm a Marxist . . .

ANDERSON: Oh, I see.

MCKENDRICK: . . . I don't mean I'm an apologist for everything done in the name of Marxism.

ANDERSON: No, no quite. There's nothing anti-socialist about it. Quite the reverse. The rich have always had it to themselves.

MCKENDRICK: On the contrary. That's why I'd be really very interested in any extra-curricular activities which might be going. I have an open mind about it.

ANDERSON: (*His wires crossed*) Oh, yes, indeed, so have I.

MCKENDRICK: I sail pretty close to the wind, Marx-wise.

ANDERSON: Mind you, it's an odd thing but travel broadens the mind in a way that the proverbialist didn't quite intend. It's only at airports and railway stations that one finds in oneself a curiosity about er—er—erotica, um, girly magazines.

(MCKENDRICK *realizes that they've had their wires crossed.*)

MCKENDRICK: Perhaps you've come across some of my articles.

ANDERSON: (*Amazed and fascinated*) You mean you write for—? (*He pulls himself up and together.*) Oh—your—er articles— I'm afraid as I explained I'm not very good at keeping up with the philosophical. . . .

(MCKENDRICK *has gone back to his former seat to fish about in his briefcase. He emerges with another girly magazine and hands it along the aisle to* ANDERSON.)

MCKENDRICK: I've got one here. Page sixty-one. The Science Fiction short story. Not a bad life. Science Fiction and sex. And, of course, the philosophical assumptions of social science.

ANDERSON: (*Faintly*) Thank you very much.

MCKENDRICK: Keep it by all means.

(ANDERSON *cautiously thumbs through pages of naked women.*) I wonder if there'll be any decent women?

2. INT. HOTEL LOBBY. PRAGUE

We are near the reception desk. ANDERSON, MCKENDRICK *and* CHETWYN *have just arrived together. Perhaps with other people. Their luggage consists only of small overnight suitcases and briefcases.*

MCKENDRICK *is at the desk half-way through his negotiations. The lobby ought to be rather large, with lifts, etc. It should be large enough to make inconspicuous a* MAN *who is carefully watching the three Englishmen. This* MAN *is aged thirty-five or younger. He is poorly dressed, but not tramp-like. His name is* PAVEL HOLLAR. *The lobby contains other people and a poorly equipped news-stand.*

We catch up with ANDERSON *talking to* CHETWYN.

ANDERSON (*Enthusiastically*) Birmingham! Excellent university. Some very good people.

(*The desk* CLERK *comes to the counter where* MCKENDRICK *is first in the queue. The* CLERK *and other Czech people in this script obviously speak with an accent but there is no attempt here to reproduce it.*)

CLERK: Third floor. Dr McKendrick.

MCKENDRICK: Only of philosophy.

CLERK: Your baggage is there?

MCKENDRICK: (*Hastily*) Oh, I'll see to that. Can I have the key, please?

CLERK: Third floor. Dr Anderson. Ninth floor. A letter for you.

(*The* CLERK *gives* ANDERSON *a sealed envelope and also a key.* ANDERSON *seems to have been expecting the letter. He thanks the* CLERK *and takes it.*)

Dr Chetwyn ninth floor.

(*The three philosophers walk towards the lifts.* PAVEL *watches them go. When they reach the lift* ANDERSON *glances round and sees two men some way off across the lobby, perhaps at the news-stand. These men are called* CRISP *and* BROADBENT. CRISP *look very young, he is twenty-two. He wears a very smart, slightly flashy suit and tie.* BROADBENT *balding but young, in his thirties. He wears flannels and a blazer.* CRISP *is quite small.* BROADBENT *is big and heavy. But both look fit.*)

ANDERSON: I say, look who's over there . . . Broadbent and Crisp.

(*The lift now opens before them.* ANDERSON *goes in showing his key to the middle-aged* WOMAN *in charge of the lift.*

MCKENDRICK *and* CHETWYN *do likewise. Over this:*)

CHETWYN: Who? (*He sees them and recognizes them.*) Oh yes.

MCKENDRICK: (*Sees them.*) Who?

CHETWYN: Crisp and Broadbent. They must be staying here too.

MCKENDRICK: Crisp? Broadbent? That kid over by the news-stand?

ANDERSON: That's Crisp.

MCKENDRICK: My God, they get younger all the time.

(*The lift doors close.*

Inside the lift.)

ANDERSON: Crisp is twenty-two. Broadbent is past his peak but Crisp is the next genius in my opinion.

MCKENDRICK: Do you know him?

ANDERSON: Not personally. I've been watching him for a couple of years.

CHETWYN: He's Newcastle, isn't he?

ANDERSON: Yes.

MCKENDRICK: I've never heard of him. What's his role there?

ANDERSON: He's what used to be called left wing. Broadbent's in the centre. He's an opportunist more than anything.

(*The lift has stopped at the third floor.*)

(*To* MCKENDRICK.) This is you—see you later.

(MCKENDRICK *steps out of the lift and looks round.*)

MCKENDRICK: Do you think the rooms are bugged?

(*The lift doors shut him off.*

Inside the lift. ANDERSON *and* CHETWYN *ride up in silence for a few moments.*)

ANDERSON: What was it Aristotle said about the higher you go
the further you fall . . . ?

CHETWYN: He was talking about tragic heroes.

(*The lift stops at the ninth floor.* ANDERSON *and* CHETWYN
leave the lift.)

I'm this way. There's a restaurant downstairs. The menu is
very limited but it's all right.

ANDERSON: You've been here before?

CHETWYN: Yes. Perhaps see you later then, sir.

(CHETWYN *goes down a corridor away from* ANDERSON'*s
corridor.*)

ANDERSON: (*To himself*) Sir?

(ANDERSON *follows the arrow towards his own room number.*)

3. INT. ANDERSON'S HOTEL ROOM

*The room contains a bed, a wardrobe, a chest. A telephone. A bath-
room containing a bath leads off through a door.*

ANDERSON *is unpacking. He puts some clothes into a drawer and closes
it. His suitcase is open on the bed.* ANDERSON *turns his attention to his
briefcase and brings out* MCKENDRICK'*s magazine. He looks round
wondering what to do with it. There is a knock on the door.* ANDERSON
*tosses the girly magazine into his suitcase and closes the case. He goes to
open the door. The caller is* PAVEL HOLLAR.

ANDERSON: Yes?

HOLLAR: I am Pavel Hollar.

ANDERSON: Yes?

HOLLAR: Professor Anderson.

(HOLLAR *is Czech and speaks with an accent.*)

ANDERSON: Hollar? Oh, heavens, yes. How extraordinary. Come
in.

HOLLAR: Thank you. I'm sorry to—

ANDERSON: No, no—what a pleasant surprise. I've only just
arrived as you can see. Sit where you can. How are you?
What are you doing? You live in Prague?

HOLLAR: Oh yes.

(ANDERSON *closes the door.*)

ANDERSON: Well, well. Well, well, well, well. How are you?
Must be ten years.

HOLLAR: Yes. It is ten. I took my degree in sixty-seven.

ANDERSON: You got a decent degree, too, didn't you?

HOLLAR: Yes, I got a first.

ANDERSON: Of course you did. Well done, well done. Are you still in philosophy?

HOLLAR: No, unfortunately.

ANDERSON: Ah. What are you doing now?

HOLLAR: I am a what do you say—a cleaner.

ANDERSON: (*With intelligent interest*) A cleaner? What is that?

HOLLAR: (*Surprised*) Cleaning. Washing. With a brush and a bucket. I am a cleaner at the bus station.

ANDERSON: You wash buses?

HOLLAR: No, not buses—the lavatories, the floors where people walk and so on.

ANDERSON: Oh. I see. You're a *cleaner*.

HOLLAR: Yes.

(*Pause.*)

ANDERSON: Are you married now, or anything?

HOLLAR: Yes. I married. She was almost my fiancée when I went to England. Irma. She is a country girl. No English. No philosophy. We have a son who is Sacha. That is Alexander.

ANDERSON: I see.

HOLLAR: And Mrs Anderson?

ANDERSON: She died. Did you meet her ever?

HOLLAR: No.

ANDERSON: (*Pause*) I don't know what to say.

HOLLAR: Did she die recently?

ANDERSON: No, I mean—a cleaner.

HOLLAR: I had one year graduate research. My doctorate studies were on certain connections with Thomas Paine and Locke. But then, since sixty-nine. . . .

ANDERSON: Cleaning lavatories.

HOLLAR: First I was in a bakery. Later on construction, building houses. Many other things. It is the way it is for many people.

ANDERSON: Is it all right for you to be here talking to me?

HOLLAR: Of course. Why not? You are my old professor.

(HOLLAR *is carrying a bag or briefcase. He puts this down and opens it.*)

I have something here.

(*From the bag he takes out the sort of envelope which would contain about thirty type-written foolscap pages. He also takes out a child's 'magic eraser' pad, the sort of pad on which one scratches a message and then slides it out to erase it.*)

You understand these things of course?

ANDERSON: (*Nonplussed*) Er . . .

HOLLAR: (*Smiling*) Of course.

(HOLLAR *demonstrates the pad briefly, then writes on the pad while Anderson watches.*)

ANDERSON: (*Stares at him*) To England?

(HOLLAR *abandons the use of the pad, and whispers in* ANDERSON's *ear.*)

HOLLAR: Excuse me.

(HOLLAR *goes to the door and opens it for* ANDERSON. HOLLAR *carries his envelope but leaves his bag in the room.* ANDERSON *goes out of the door baffled.* HOLLAR *follows him. They walk a few paces down the corridor.*)

Thank you. It is better to be careful.

ANDERSON: Why? You don't seriously suggest that my room is bugged?

HOLLAR: It is better to assume it.

ANDERSON: Why?

(*Just then the door of the room next to* ANDERSON's *opens and a* MAN *comes out. He is about forty and wears a dark rather shapeless suit. He glances at* ANDERSON *and* HOLLAR. *And then walks off in the opposite direction towards the lifts and passes out of sight.* HOLLAR *and* ANDERSON *instinctively pause until the* MAN *has gone.*)

I hope you're not getting me into trouble.

HOLLAR: I hope not. I don't think so. I have friends in trouble.

ANDERSON: I know, it's dreadful—but . . . well, what is it?

(HOLLAR *indicates his envelope.*)

HOLLAR: My doctoral thesis. It is mainly theoretical. Only ten thousand words, but very formally arranged.

ANDERSON: My goodness . . . ten years in the writing.

HOLLAR: No. I wrote it this month—when I heard of this congress here and you coming. I decided. Everyday in the night.

53

ANDERSON: Of course. I'd be very happy to read it.

HOLLAR: It is in Czech.

ANDERSON: Oh . . . well . . . ?

HOLLAR: I'm afraid so. But Peter Volkansky—he was with me, you remember—we came together in sixty-three—

ANDERSON: Oh yes—Volkansky—yes, I do remember him. He never came back here.

HOLLAR: No. He didn't come back. He was a realist.

ANDERSON: He's at Reading or somewhere like that.

HOLLAR: Lyster.

ANDERSON: Leicester. Exactly. Are you in touch with him?

HOLLAR: A little. He will translate it and try to have it published in English. If it's good. I think it is good.

ANDERSON: But can't you publish it in Czech? . . . (*This catches up on him and he shakes his head.*) Oh, Hollar . . . now, you know, really, I'm a guest of the government here.

HOLLAR: They would not search you.

ANDERSON: That's not the point. I'm sorry . . . I mean it would be bad manners, wouldn't it?

HOLLAR: Bad manners?

ANDERSON: I know it sounds rather lame. But ethics and manners are interestingly related. The history of human calumny is largely a series of breaches of good manners. . . . (*Pause.*) Perhaps if I said correct behaviour it wouldn't sound so ridiculous. You do see what I mean. I am sorry. . . . Look, can we go back . . . I ought to unpack.

HOLLAR: My thesis is about correct behaviour.

ANDERSON: Oh yes?

HOLLAR: Here you know, individual correctness is defined by what is correct for the State.

ANDERSON: Yes, I know.

HOLLAR: I ask how collective right can have meaning by itself. I ask where it comes from, the idea of a collective ethic.

ANDERSON: Yes.

HOLLAR: I reply, it comes from the individual. One man's dealings with another man.

ANDERSON: Yes.

HOLLAR: The collective ethic can only be the individual ethic writ big.

ANDERSON: Writ large.

HOLLAR: Writ large, precisely. The ethics of the State must be judged against the fundamental ethic of the individual. The human being, not the citizen. I conclude there is an obligation, a human responsibility, to fight against the State correctness. Unfortunately that is not a safe conclusion.

ANDERSON: Quite. The difficulty arises when one asks oneself how the *individual* ethic can have any meaning by itself. Where does *that* come from? In what sense is it intelligible, for example, to say that a man has certain inherent, individual rights? It is much easier to understand how a community of individuals can decide to give each other certain rights. These rights may or may not include, for example, the right to publish something. In that situation, the individual ethic would flow from the collective ethic, just as the State says it does.

(*Pause.*)

I only mean it is a question you would have to deal with.

HOLLAR: I mean, it is not safe for me.

ANDERSON: (*Still misunderstanding*) Well yes, but for example, you could say that such an arrangement between a man and the State is a sort of contract, and it is the essence of a contract that both parties enter into it freely. And you have not entered into it freely. I mean, that would be one line of attack.

HOLLAR: It is not the main line. You see, to me the idea of an inherent right is intelligible. I believe that we have such rights, and they are paramount.

ANDERSON: Yes, I see you do, but how do you justify the assertion?

HOLLAR: I observe. I observe my son for example.

ANDERSON: Your son?

HOLLAR: For example.

(*Pause.*)

ANDERSON: Look, there's no need to stand out here. There's . . . no point. I was going to have a bath and change . . . meeting some of my colleagues later. . . .

(ANDERSON *moves to go but* HOLLAR *stops him with a touch on the arm.*)

55

HOLLAR: I am not a famous dissident. A writer, a scientist. . . .

ANDERSON: No.

HOLLAR: If I am picked up—on the way home, let us say—there is no fuss. A cleaner. I will be one of hundreds. It's all right. In the end it must change. But I have something to say—that is all. If I leave my statement behind, then it's O.K. You understand?

ANDERSON: Perhaps the correct thing for me to have done is not to have accepted their invitation to speak here. But I did accept it. It is a contract, as it were, freely entered into. And having accepted their hospitality I cannot in all conscience start smuggling. . . . It's just not ethical.

HOLLAR: But if you didn't know you were smuggling it—

ANDERSON: Smuggling entails knowledge.

HOLLAR: If I hid my thesis in your luggage, for instance.

ANDERSON: That's childish. Also, you could be getting me into trouble, and your quarrel is not with me. Your action would be unethical on your own terms—one man's dealings with another man. I am sorry.

(ANDERSON *goes back towards his door, which* HOLLAR *had left ajar.* HOLLAR *follows him.*)

HOLLAR: No, it is I who must apologize.

The man next door, is he one of your group?

ANDERSON: No. I don't know him.

(ANDERSON *opens his bedroom door. He turns as if to say good-bye.*)

HOLLAR: My bag.

ANDERSON: Oh yes.

(HOLLAR *follows* ANDERSON *into the room.*)

HOLLAR: You will have a bath . . . ?

ANDERSON: I thought I would.

(HOLLAR *turns into the bathroom.* ANDERSON *stays in the bedroom, surprised.*

He hears the bath water being turned on. The bath water makes a rush of sound. ANDERSON *enters the bathroom and sees* HOLLAR *sitting on the edge of the bath.*

Interior bathroom.)

HOLLAR: (*Quietly*) I have not yet made a copy.

ANDERSON: (*Loudly*) What?

56

(HOLLAR *goes up to* ANDERSON *and speaks close to* ANDERSON'*s ear. The bath taps make a loud background noise*.)

HOLLAR: I have not yet made a copy. I have a bad feeling about carrying this home. (*He indicates his envelope*.) I did not expect to take it away. I ask a favour. (*Smiles*.) Ethical.

ANDERSON: (*Quietly now*) What is it?

HOLLAR: Let me leave this here and you can bring it to my apartment tomorrow—I have a safe place for it there.
(HOLLAR *takes a piece of paper and a pencil from his pocket and starts writing his address in capital letters*.)

ANDERSON: But you know my time here is very crowded—
(*Then he gives in*.) Do you live nearby?

HOLLAR: It is not far. I have written my address.
(HOLLAR *gives* ANDERSON *the paper*.)

ANDERSON: (*Forgetting to be quiet*) Do you seriously—
(HOLLAR *quietens* ANDERSON.)
Do you seriously expect to be searched on the way home?

HOLLAR: I don't know, but it is better to be careful. I wrote a letter to Mr Husak. Also some other things. So sometimes they follow me.

ANDERSON: But you weren't worried about bringing the thesis with you.

HOLLAR: No. If anybody watches me they want to know what books *you* give *me*.

ANDERSON: I see. Yes, all right, Hollar. I'll bring it tomorrow.

HOLLAR: Please don't leave it in your room when you go to eat. Take your briefcase.
(*They go back into the bedroom*. ANDERSON *puts* HOLLAR'*s envelope into his briefcase*.)
(*Normal voice*) So perhaps you will come and meet my wife.

ANDERSON: Yes. Should I telephone?

HOLLAR: Unfortunately my telephone is removed. I am home all day. Saturday.

ANDERSON: Oh yes.

HOLLAR: Good-bye.

ANDERSON: Good-bye.
(HOLLAR *goes to the door carrying his bag*.)

HOLLAR: I forgot—welcome to Prague.
(HOLLAR *leaves closing the door*.

57

ANDERSON *stands still for a few moments. Then he hears footsteps approaching down the corridor. The footsteps appear to stop outside his room. But then the door to the next room is opened and the unseen man enters the room next door and loudly closes the door behind him.*)

4. INT. ANDERSON'S ROOM. MORNING.

Close-up of the colloquium brochure. It is lying on ANDERSON's *table. Then* ANDERSON *picks it up. His dress and appearance, and the light outside the window, tell us that it is morning. Dressed to go out,* ANDERSON *picks up his briefcase and leaves the room.*

In the corridor he walks towards the lifts.

At the lifts he finds CRISP *waiting.* ANDERSON *stands next to* CRISP *silently for a few moments.*

ANDERSON: Good morning. (*Pause.*) Mr Crisp . . . my name is Anderson. I'm a very great admirer of yours.

CRISP: (*Chewing gum*) Oh . . . ta.

ANDERSON: Good luck this afternoon.

CRISP: Thanks. Bloody useless, the lifts in this place.

ANDERSON: Are you all staying in this hotel?

(CRISP *doesn't seem to hear this.* CRISP *sees* BROADBENT *emerging from a room.* BROADBENT *carries a zipped bag,* CRISP *has a similar bag.*)

CRISP: (*Shouts*) Here you are, Roy—it's waiting for you.

(BROADBENT *arrives.*)

ANDERSON: Good morning. Good luck this afternoon.

BROADBENT: Right. Thanks. Are you over for the match?

ANDERSON: Yes. Well, partly. I've got my ticket.

(ANDERSON *takes out of his pocket the envelope he received from the hotel* CLERK *and shows it.*)

CRISP: (*Quietly*) You didn't pull her, then?

BROADBENT: No chance.

CRISP: They don't trust you, do they?

BROADBENT: Well, they're right, aren't they? Remember Milan.

CRISP: (*Laughing*) Yeah—

(*The bell sounds to indicate that the lift is arriving.*)

About bloody time.

ANDERSON: I see from yesterday's paper that they've brought in Jirasek for Vladislav.

BROADBENT: Yes, that's right. Six foot eight, they say.

ANDERSON: He's not very good in the air unless he's got lots of space.

(BROADBENT *looks at him curiously. The lift doors open and the three of them get in. There is no one else in the lift except the female* OPERATOR.
Interior lift.)

BROADBENT: You've seen him, have you?

ANDERSON: I've seen him twice. In the UFA Cup a few seasons ago. . . . I happened to be in Berlin for the Hegel Colloquium, er, bunfight. And then last season I was in Bratislava to receive an honorary degree.

CRISP: Tap his ankles for him. Teach him to be six foot eight.

BROADBENT: Leave off— (*He nods at the lift* OPERATOR.) You never know, do you?

CRISP: Yeah, maybe the lift's bugged.

ANDERSON: He scored both times from the same move, and came close twice more—

BROADBENT: Oh yes?

(*Pause.*)

ANDERSON: (*In a rush*) I realize it's none of my business—I mean you may think I'm an absolute ass, but—
(*Pause.*)
Look, if Halas takes a corner he's going to make it short—almost certainly—push it back to Deml or Kautsky, who pulls the defence out. Jirasek hangs about for the chip to the far post. They'll do the same thing from a set piece. Three or four times in the same match. *Really.* Short corners and free kicks.

(*The lift stops at the third floor.* BROADBENT *and* CRISP *are staring at* ANDERSON.)

(*Lamely.*) Anyway, that's why they've brought Jirasek back, in my opinion.

(*The lift doors open and* MCKENDRICK *gets in.* MCKENDRICK's *manner is breezy and bright.*)

MCKENDRICK: Good morning! You've got together then?

ANDERSON: A colleague. Mr McKendrick . . .

MCKENDRICK: You're Crisp. (*He takes* CRISP's *hand and shakes it.*)
Bill McKendrick. I hear you're doing some very interesting

work in Newcastle. Great stuff. I still like to think of myself
as a bit of a left-winger at Stoke. Of course, my stuff is
largely empirical—I leave epistemologial questions to the
scholastics—eh, Anderson? (*He pokes* ANDERSON *in the ribs.*)

ANDERSON: McKendrick . . .

BROADBENT: Did you say *Stoke*?

(*The lift arives at the ground floor.*)

MCKENDRICK: (*To* BROADBENT) We've met, haven't we? Your face
is familiar . . .

(BROADBENT, CRISP *and* MCKENDRICK *in close attendance leave
the lift.* ANDERSON *is slow on the uptake but follows.*)

ANDERSON: McKendrick—?

MCKENDRICK: (*Prattling*) There's a choice of open forums tonight
—neo-Hegelians or Quinian neo-Positivists. Which do you
fancy? Pity Quine couldn't be here. And Hegel for that
matter.

(MCKENDRICK *laughs brazenly in the lobby.* BROADBENT *and*
CRISP *eye him warily.* ANDERSON *winces.*)

5. INT. THE COLLOQUIUM

*The general idea is that a lot of philosophers sit in a sort of theatre
while on stage one of their number reads a paper from behind a lectern,
with a* CHAIRMAN *in attendance behind him. The set up however is quite
complicated. To one side are three glassed-in booths, each one containing
'simultaneous interpreters'. These interpreters have earphones and
microphones. They also have a copy of the lecture being given. One of
these interpreters is translating into Czech, another into French,
another into German. The audience is furnished either with earphones or
with those hand-held phones which are issued in theatres sometimes.
Each of these phones can tune into any of the three interpreters depending
upon the language of the listener. For our purposes it is better to have the
hand-held phones.*

It is important to the play, specifically to a later scene when ANDERSON
is talking, that the hall and the audience should be substantial.

At the moment ANDERSON *is in the audience, sitting next to* MCKENDRICK.
MCKENDRICK *is still discomforted.* CHETWYN *is elsewhere in the
audience.*

*We begin however with a large close-up of the speaker who is an
American called* STONE. *After the first sentence or two of* STONE's *speech,*

the camera will acquaint us with the situation. At different points during STONE's *speech, there is conversation between* ANDERSON *and* MCKENDRICK. *In this script, these conversations are placed immediately after that part of* STONE's *speech which they will cover. This applies also to any other interpolations. Obviously,* STONE *does not pause to let these other things in.*

STONE: The confusion which often arises from the ambiguity of ordinary language raises special problems for a logical language. This is especially so when the ambiguity is not casual and inadvertent—but when it's contrived. In fact, the limitations of a logical language are likely to appear when we ask ourselves whether it can accommodate a literature, or whether poetry can be reduced to a logical language. It is here that deliberate ambiguity for effect makes problems.

ANDERSON: Perfectly understandable mistake.

STONE: Nor must we confuse ambiguity, furthermore, with mere synonymity. When we say that a politician ran for office, that is not an ambiguous statement, it is merely an instance of a word having different applications, literal, idiomatic and so on.

MCKENDRICK: I said I knew his face.

ANDERSON: Match of the Day.

STONE: The intent is clear in each application. The show ran well on Broadway. Native Dancer ran well at Kentucky, and so on. (*In the audience a Frenchman expresses dismay and bewilderment as his earphones give out a literal translation of 'a native dancer' running well at Kentucky. Likewise a German listener has the same problem.*)
And what about this word 'Well'? Again, it is applied as a qualifier with various intent—the show ran for a long time, the horse ran fast, and so on.

MCKENDRICK: So this pressing engagement of yours is a football match.

ANDERSON: A World Cup qualifier is not just a football match.

STONE: Again, there is no problem here so long as these variations are what I propose to call reliable. 'You eat well' says Mary to John, 'You cook well' says John to Mary. We know that when Mary says 'You *eat* well' she does not mean that John eats *skilfully*. Just as we know that when John says 'You cook

61

well' he does not mean that Mary cooks *abundantly*.

ANDERSON: But I'm sorry about missing your paper, I really am.

STONE: I say that we know this, but I mean only that our general experience indicates it. The qualifier takes its meaning from the contexual force of the verb it qualifies. But it is the mark of a sound theory that it should take account not merely of our general experience, but also of the particular experience, and not merely of the particular experience but also of the unique experience, and not merely of the unique experience but also of the hypothetical experience. It is when we consider the world of *possibilities*, hypothetical experience, that we get closer to ambiguity. 'You cook well' says John to Mary. 'You eat well' says Mary to John.

MCKENDRICK: Do you ever wonder whether all this is worthwhile?

ANDERSON: No.

MCKENDRICK: I know what you mean.

(CHETWYN *is twisting the knob on his translation phone, to try all this out in different languages. He is clearly bored. He looks at his watch.*)

STONE: No problems there. But I ask you to imagine a competition when what is being judged is table manners.

(*Insert* FRENCH INTERPRETER's *box—interior.*)

INTERPRETER: . . . bonne tenue *à* table . . .

STONE: John enters this competition and afterwards Mary says, 'Well, you certainly ate well!' Now Mary seems to be saying that John ate *skilfully—with refinement*. And again, I ask you to imagine a competition where the amount of food eaten is taken into account along with refinement of table manners. *Now* Mary says to John, 'Well, you didn't eat very well, but at least you ate well.'

INTERPRETER: Alors, vous n'avez pas bien mangé . . . mais . . .

(*All* INTERPRETERS *baffled by this.*)

STONE: Now clearly there is no way to tell whether Mary means that John ate abundantly but clumsily, or that John ate frugally but elegantly. Here we have a genuine ambiguity. To restate Mary's sentence in a logical language we would have to ask her what she meant.

MCKENDRICK: By the way, I've got you a copy of my paper.

ANDERSON: Oh, many thanks.

MCKENDRICK: It's not a long paper. You could read it comfortably during half-time.

(MCKENDRICK *gives* ANDERSON *his paper*.)

STONE: But this is to assume that Mary exists. Let us say she is a fictitious character in a story I have written. Very well, you say to me, the author, 'What did Mary mean?' Well I might reply—'I don't know what she meant. Her ambiguity makes the necessary point of my story.' And here I think the idea of a logical language which can *only* be unambiguous, breaks down.

(ANDERSON *opens his briefcase and puts* MCKENDRICK's *paper into it. He fingers* HOLLAR's *envelope and broods over it.*
STONE *has concluded. He sits down to applause. The* CHAIRMAN, *who has been sitting behind him has stood up.*)

ANDERSON: I'm going to make a discreet exit—I've got a call to make before the match.

(ANDERSON *stands up*.)

CHAIRMAN: Yes—Professor Anderson I think . . . ?

(ANDERSON *is caught like a rabbit in the headlights.* MCKENDRICK *enjoys his predicament and becomes interested in how* ANDERSON *will deal with it.*)

ANDERSON: Ah . . . I would only like to offer Professor Stone the observation that language is not the only level of human communication, and perhaps not the most important level. Whereof we cannot speak, thereof we are by no means silent.

(MCKENDRICK *smiles* 'Bravo'.)

Verbal language is a technical refinement of our capacity for communication, rather than the *fons et origo* of that capacity. The likelihood is that language develops in an *ad hoc* way, so there is no reason to expect its development to be logical. (*A thought strikes him.*) The importance of language is overrated. It allows me and Professor Stone to show off a bit, and it is very useful for communicating detail—but the important truths are simple and monolithic. The essentials of a given situation speak for themselves, and language is as capable of obscuring the truth as of revealing it. Thank you.

(ANDERSON *edges his way out towards the door*.)

CHAIRMAN: (*Uncertainly*) Professor Stone . . .

STONE: Well, what was the question?

6. EXT. FRONT DOOR OF THE HOLLAR APARTMENT

The apartment is one of two half-way up a large old building. The stairwell is dirty and uncared for. The HOLLAR *front door is on a landing, and the front door of another flat is across the landing. Stairs go up and down.* ANDERSON *comes up the stairs and finds the right number on the door and rings the bell. He is carrying his briefcase.*

All the men in this scene are Czech plainclothes POLICEMEN. *They will be identified in this text merely by number.* MAN 3 *is the one in charge. Man 1 comes to the door.*

ANDERSON: I'm looking for Mr Hollar.

> (MAN 1 *shakes his head. He looks behind him.* MAN 2 *comes to the door.*)

MAN 2: (*In Czech*) Yes? Who are you?

ANDERSON: English? Um. Parlez-vous francais? Er. Spreckanzydoitch?

MAN 2: (*In German*) Deutch? Ein Bischen.

ANDERSON: Actually I don't. Does Mr Hollar live here? Apartment Hollar?

> (MAN 2 *speaks to somebody behind him.*)

MAN 2: (*In Czech*) An Englishman. Do you know him?

> (MRS HOLLAR *comes to the door. She is about the same age as* HOLLAR.)

ANDERSON: Mrs Hollar?

> (MRS HOLLAR *nods.*)

Is your husband here? Pavel . . .

MRS HOLLAR: (*In Czech*) Pavel is arrested.

> (*Inside, behind the door,* MAN 3 *is heard shouting, in Czech.*)

MAN 3: (*Not seen*) What's going on there?

> (MAN 3 *comes to the door.*)

ANDERSON: I am looking for Mr Hollar. I am a friend from England. His Professor. My name is Anderson.

MAN 3. (*In English*) Not here. (*In Czech to* MRS HOLLAR.) He says he is a friend of your husband. Anderson.

ANDERSON: He was my student.

> (MRS HOLLAR *calls out.*)

MAN 3: (*In Czech*) Shut up.

ANDERSON: Student. Philosophy.

> (MRS HOLLAR *calls out.*)

MAN 3: Shut up.

(MAN 3 *and* MAN 2 *come out of the flat on to the landing,*
closing the door behind them.)

ANDERSON: I just came to see him. Just to say hello. For a
minute. I have a taxi waiting. Taxi.

MAN 3: Taxi.

ANDERSON: Yes. I can't stay.

MAN 3: (*In English*) Moment. O.K.

ANDERSON: I can't stay.

(MAN 3 *rings the bell of the adjacent flat. A rather scared*
woman opens the door. MAN 3 *asks, in Czech, to use the phone.*
MAN 3 *goes inside the other flat.* ANDERSON *begins to realize*
the situation.)

Well, look, if you don't mind—I'm on my way to—an
engagement. . . .

MAN 2: (*In Czech*) Stay here.

(*Pause.* ANDERSON *looks at his watch. Then from inside the flat*
MRS HOLLAR *is shouting in Czech.*)

MRS HOLLAR: (*Unseen*) I'm entitled to a witness of my choice.

(*The door is opened violently and immediately slammed.*
ANDERSON *becomes agitated.*)

ANDERSON: What's going on in there?

MAN 2: (*In Czech*) Stay here, he won't be a minute.

(ANDERSON *can hear* MRS HOLLAR *shouting.*)

ANDERSON: Now look here—

(ANDERSON *rings the doorbell.*
The door is opened by MAN 4.)

I demand to speak to Mrs Hollar.

(*Upstairs and downstairs doors are opening and people are*
shouting, in Czech 'What's going on?' And so on. There is also
shouting from inside the flat. MAN 2 *shouts up and down the*
staircase, in Czech.)

MAN 2: (*In Czech*) Go inside!

ANDERSON: Now look here, I am the J. S. Mill Professor of
Ethics at the University of Cambridge and I demand that I
am allowed to leave or to telephone the British Ambassador!

MAN 4: (*In Czech*) Bring him inside.

MAN 2: (*In Czech*) In.

(*He pushes* ANDERSON *into the flat. Interior flat. The hallway.*
Inside it is apparent that the front door leads to more than one

flat. Off the very small dirty hall there is a kitchen, a lavatory and two other doors, not counting the door to the HOLLAR *rooms.)*

MAN 4: (*In Czech*) Stay with him.

(*The* HOLLAR *interior door is opened from inside by* MRS HOLLAR.)

MRS HOLLAR: (*In Czech*) If he's my witness he's allowed in here.

MAN 4: (*In Czech*) Go inside—he's not your witness.

(MAN 4 *pushes* MRS HOLLAR *inside and closes the door from within. This leaves* ANDERSON *and* MAN 2 *in the little hall. Another door now opens, and a small girl, poorly dressed, looks round it. She is jerked back out of sight by someone and the door is pulled closed. The* HOLLAR *door is flung open again, by* MRS HOLLAR.)

MRS HOLLAR: (*In Czech*) I want this door open.

MAN 2: (*In Czech*) Leave it open then. He'll be back in a minute.

(MAN 4 *disappears back inside the flat.* MRS HOLLAR *is heard.*)

MRS HOLLAR: (*Unseen. In Czech*) Bastards.

(ANDERSON *stands in the hallway. He can hear* MRS HOLLAR *starting to cry.* ANDERSON *looks completely out of his depth.*)

ANDERSON: My God. . . .

(*Then the doorbell rings.* MAN 2 *opens it to let in* MAN 3.)

MAN 2: (*In Czech*) We had to come in to shut her up.

MAN 3: (*In Czech*) Well, he's coming over. (*In English to* ANDERSON.) Captain coming. Speak English.

ANDERSON: I would like to telephone the British Ambassador.

MAN 3: (*In English*) O.K. Captain coming.

ANDERSON: How long will he be? I have an appointment. (*He looks at his watch.*) Yes, by God! I do have an engagement and it starts in half an hour—

MAN 3: (*In English*) Please.

(*A lavatory flushes. From the other interior door an* OLD MAN *comes out.* MAN 3 *nods curtly at the* OLD MAN. *The* OLD MAN *shuffles by looking at* ANDERSON. MAN 3 *becomes uneasy at being in the traffic. He decides to bring* ANDERSON *inside the flat. He does so.*

Interior HOLLAR's *room. There are two connecting rooms. Beyond this room is a door leading to a bedroom. This door is open. The rooms seem full of people. The rooms are small and shabby. They are being thoroughly searched, and obviously have been in this process for hours. The searchers do not spoil or destroy anything. There are no torn cushions or anything like that. However, the floor of the first room is almost covered in books. The bookcases which line perhaps two of the walls are empty. The rug could be rolled up, and there could be one or two floorboards up.*

MAN 1 *is going through the books, leafing through each one and looking along the spine. He is starting to put books back on the shelves one by one.* MAN 5 *has emptied drawers of their contents and is going through a pile of papers.* MRS HOLLAR *stands in the doorway between the two rooms. Beyond her* MAN 2 *can be seen searching.* [MAN 4 *is out of sight in the bedroom.*] MAN 3 *indicates a chair on which* ANDERSON *should sit.* ANDERSON *sits putting his briefcase on the floor by his feet. He looks around. He sees a clock showing 2.35.*

Mix to clock showing 2.55.

ANDERSON *is where he was.* MAN 1 *is still on the books.* MAN 5 *is still looking through papers.* MAN 3 *is examining the inside of a radio set.*

Voices are heard faintly on the stairs. There is a man remonstrating. A woman's voice too.

The doorbell rings.

MAN 3 *leaves the room, closing the door.* ANDERSON *hears him go to the front door. There is some conversation. The front door closes again and* MAN 3 *re-enters the room.*)

MAN 3: (*In English to* ANDERSON) Taxi.

ANDERSON: Oh—I forgot him. Dear me.

MAN 3: O.K.

ANDERSON: I must pay him.

(ANDERSON *takes out his wallet.* MAN 3 *takes it from him without snatching.*)

MAN 3: O.K.

(MAN 3 *looks through the wallet.*)

ANDERSON: Give that back— (*Furious*) Now, you listen to me— this has gone on quite long enough—I demand—to be allowed to leave. . . .

(ANDERSON *has stood up.* MAN 3 *gently pushes him back into the chair. In* ANDERSON'*s wallet* MAN 3 *finds his envelope and*

discovers the football ticket. He puts it back. He looks
sympathetically at ANDERSON.)

MAN 3: (*In Czech*) The old boy's got a ticket for the England
match. No wonder he's furious. (*He gives the wallet back to*
ANDERSON. *In English*.) Taxi O.K. No money. He go.
Football no good.

ANDERSON: Serve me right.

MAN 5: (*In Czech*) It's on the radio. Let him have it on.
(MAN 3 *returns to the radio and turns it on*.
MRS HOLLAR *enters quickly from the bedroom and turns it off*.)

MRS HOLLAR: (*In Czech*) That's my radio.

MAN 3: (*In Czech*) Your friend wants to listen to the match.
(MRS HOLLAR *looks at* ANDERSON. *She turns the radio on.*
The radio is talking about the match which is just about to
begin.)

MAN 3: (*In English*) Is good. O.K.?
(ANDERSON, *listening, realizes that the radio is listing the names*
of the English team.
Then the match begins.
Mix to:
The same situation about half an hour later. The radio is still
on. MAN 1 *is still on the books. He has put aside three or four*
English books. MAN 5 *has disappeared.* MAN 2 *is sorting out the*
fluff from a carpet sweeper. MAN 4 *is standing on a chair*
examining the inside of a ventilation grating.
ANDERSON *gets up off his chair and starts to walk towards the*
bedroom. The three MEN *in the room look up but don't stop him.*
ANDERSON *enters the bedroom.*
Interior bedroom.
MAN 3 *is going through pockets in a wardrobe.* MAN 5 *is*
looking under floorboards. MRS HOLLAR *is sitting on the bed*
watching them.)

ANDERSON: It's half-past three. I demand to be allowed to leave
or to telephone the British—

MAN 3: Please—too slow.

ANDERSON: I demand to leave—

MAN 3: O.K. Who wins football?

ANDERSON: (*Pause*) No score.
(*The doorbell goes.*

MAN 3 *goes into the other room and to the door.* ANDERSON *follows him as far as the other room. On the way through* MAN 3 *signals to turn off the radio.* MAN 2 *turns off the radio.* MRS HOLLAR *comes in and turns the radio on.*)

MRS HOLLAR: (*In Czech*) Show me where it says I can't listen to my own radio.

(MAN 3 *returns from the front door with* MAN 6. MAN 6 *enters the room saying:*)

MAN 6: (*In Czech*) I said don't let him leave—I didn't say bring him inside. (*To* ANDERSON *in English.*) Professor Anderson? I'm sorry your friend Mr Hollar has got himself into trouble.

ANDERSON: Thank Christ—now listen to me—I am a professor of philosophy. I am a guest of the Czechoslovakian government. I might almost say an honoured guest. I have been invited to speak at the Colloquium in Prague. My connections in England reach up to the highest in the land—

MAN 6: Do you know the Queen?

ANDERSON: Certainly. (*But he has rushed into that.*) No, I do not know the Queen—but I speak the truth when I say that I am personally acquainted with two members of the government, one of whom has been to my house, and I assure you that unless I am allowed to leave this building immediately there is going to be a major incident about the way my liberty has been impeded by your men. I do not know what they are doing here, I do not care what they are doing here—

MAN 6: Excuse me. Professor. There is some mistake. I thought you were here as a friend of the Hollar family.

ANDERSON: I know Pavel Hollar, certainly.

MAN 6: Absolutely. You are here as a friend, at Mrs Hollar's request.

ANDERSON: I just dropped in to—what do you mean?

MAN 6: Mr Hollar unfortunately has been arrested for a serious crime against the State. It is usual for the home of an accused person to be searched for evidence, and so on. I am sure the same thing happens in your country. Well, under our law Mrs Hollar is entitled to have a friendly witness present during the search. To be frank she is entitled to two

69

witnesses. So if, for example, an expensive vase is broken by mistake, and the police claim it was broken before, it will not just be her word against theirs. And so on. I think you will agree that's fair.

ANDERSON: Well?

MAN 6: Well, my understanding is that she asked you to be her witness. (*In Czech to* MRS HOLLAR.) Did you ask him to be your witness?

MRS HOLLAR: (*In Czech*) Yes, I did.

MAN 6: (*In English to* ANDERSON) Yes. Exactly so. (*Pause.*) You are Mr Hollar's friend, aren't you?

ANDERSON: I taught him in Cambridge after he left Czechoslovakia.

MAN 6: A brave man.

ANDERSON: Yes . . . a change of language . . . and culture . . .

MAN 6: He walked across a minefield. In 1962. Brave.

ANDERSON: Perhaps he was simply desperate.

MAN 6: Perhaps a little ungrateful. The State, you know, educated him, fed him, for eighteen years. 'Thank you very much—good-bye.'

ANDERSON: Well he came back, in the Spring of sixty-eight.

MAN 6: Oh yes.

ANDERSON: A miscalculation.

MAN 6: How do you mean?

ANDERSON: Well, really . . . there are a lot of things wrong in England but it is still not 'a serious crime against the State' to put forward a philosophical view which does not find favour with the Government.

MAN 6: Professor. . . . Hollar is charged with currency offences. There is a black market in hard currency. It is illegal. We do not have laws about philosophy. He is an ordinary criminal.

(*Pause.*

The radio commentary has continued softly. But in this pause it changes pitch. It is clear to ANDERSON, *and to us, that something particular has occurred in the match.* MAN 6 *is listening.*)

(*In English.*) Penalty. (*He listens for a moment.*) For us, I'm afraid.

ANDERSON: Yes, I can hear.

(*This is because it is clear from the crowd noise that it's a penalty for the home side.* MAN 6 *listens again.*)

MAN 6: (*In English*) Broadbent—a bad tackle when Deml had a certain goal . . . a what you call it?—a necessary foul.

ANDERSON: A professional foul.

MAN 6: Yes.

(*On the radio the goal is scored. This is perfectly clear from the the crowd reaction.*)

Not good for you.

(MAN 6 *turns off the radio. Pause.* MAN 6 *considers* ANDERSON.)

So you have had a philosophical discussion with Hollar.

ANDERSON: I believe you implied that I was free to go. (*He stands up.*) I am quite sure you know that Hollar visited me at my hotel last night. It was a social call, which I was returning when I walked into this. And furthermore, I understood nothing about being a witness—I was prevented from leaving. I only came to say hello, and meet Pavel's wife, on my way to the football—

MAN 6: (*With surprise*) So you came to Czechoslovakia to go to the football match, Professor?

(*This rattles* ANDERSON.)

ANDERSON: Certainly not. Well, the afternoon of the Colloquium was devoted to—well, it was not a condition of my invitation that I should attend all the sessions. (*Pause.*) I was invited to *speak*, not to listen. I am speaking tomorrow morning.

MAN 6: Why should I know Hollar visited you at the hotel?

ANDERSON: He told me he was often followed.

MAN 6: Well, when a man is known to be engaged in meeting foreigners to buy currency—

ANDERSON: I don't believe any of that—he was being harassed because of his letter to Husak—

MAN 6: A letter to President Husak? What sort of letter?

ANDERSON: (*Flustered*) Your people knew about it—

MAN 6: It is not a crime to write to the President—

ANDERSON: No doubt that depends on what is written.

MAN 6: You mean he wrote some kind of slander?

ANDERSON: (*Heatedly*) I insist on leaving now.

MAN 6: Of course. You know, your taxi driver has made a complaint against you.

ANDERSON: What are you talking about?

MAN 6: He never got paid.

ANDERSON: Yes, I'm sorry but—

MAN 6: You are not to blame. My officer told him to go.

ANDERSON: Yes, that's right.

MAN 6: Still, he is very unhappy. You told him you would be five minutes you were delivering something—

ANDERSON: How could I have told him that? I don't speak Czech.

MAN 6: You showed him five on your watch, and you did all the things people do when they talk to each other without a language. He was quite certain you were delivering something in your briefcase.

(*Pause.*)

ANDERSON: Yes. All right. But it was not money.

MAN 6: Of course not. You are not a criminal.

ANDERSON: Quite so. I promised to bring Pavel one or two of the Colloquium papers. He naturally has an interest in philosophy and I assume it is not illegal.

MAN 6: Naturally not. Then you won't mind showing me.

(ANDERSON *hesitates then opens the briefcase and takes out* MCKENDRICK's *paper and his own and passes them over.* MAN 6 *takes them and reads their English titles.*)

'Ethical Fictions as Ethical Foundations' . . . 'Philosophy and the Catastrophe Theory'.

(MAN 6 *gives the papers back to* ANDERSON.)

MAN 6: You wish to go to the football match? You will see twenty minutes, perhaps more.

ANDERSON: No. I'm going back to the university, to the Colloquium.

MRS HOLLAR: (*In Czech*) Is he leaving?

MAN 6: Mrs Hollar would like you to remain.

ANDERSON: (*To* MRS HOLLAR) No, I'm sorry. (*A thought strikes him.*) If you spoke to the taxi driver you would have known perfectly well I was going to the England match.

(MAN 6 *doesn't reply to this either in word or expression.* ANDERSON *closes his briefcase.*

The doorbell rings and MAN 3 *goes to open the door.*

From the bedroom MAN 5 *enters with a small parcel wrapped*

72

in old newspaper.)

MAN 5: (*In Czech*) I found this, Chief, under the floorboards.
(MAN 5 *gives the parcel to* MAN 6 *who unwraps it to reveal a
bundle of American dollars.*

MRS HOLLAR *watches this with disbelief and there is an
outburst.*)

MRS HOLLAR: (*In Czech*) He's lying! (*To* ANDERSON.) It's a lie—
The door reopens for MAN 3. SACHA HOLLAR, *aged ten, comes
in with him. He is rather a tough little boy. He runs across to
his mother, who is crying and shouting, and embraces her. It is
rather as though he were a small adult comforting her.*)

ANDERSON: Oh my God . . . Mrs Hollar . . .
(ANDERSON, *out of his depth and afraid, decides abruptly to
leave and does so.* MAN 3 *isn't sure whether to let him go but*
MAN 6 *nods at him and* ANDERSON *leaves.*)

7. INT. HOTEL CORRIDOR. EVENING

ANDERSON *approaches his room. He is worn out. When he gets to his
door and fumbles with his key he realizes that he can hear a voice in
the room next door to his. He puts his ear to this other door.*

GRAYSON: (*Inside*) Yes, a new top for the running piece—O.K.—
Prague, Saturday.
(GRAYSON *speaks not particularly slowly but with great
deliberation enunciating every consonant and splitting syllables
up where necessary for clarity. He is, of course, dictating to a
fast typist.*)
There'll be Czechs bouncing in the streets of Prague tonight
as bankruptcy stares English football in the face, stop, new
par.
(ANDERSON *knocks on the door.*)
(*Inside.*) It's open!
(ANDERSON *opens the door and looks into the room.
Interior room. It is of course a room very like* ANDERSON's *own
room, if not identical. Its occupant, the man we had seen leave
the room earlier is* GRAYSON, *a sports reporter from England.
He is on the telephone as* ANDERSON *cautiously enters the room.*)
Make no mistake, comma, the four-goal credit which these
slick Slovaks netted here this afternoon will keep them in the
black through the second leg of the World Cup Eliminator

at Wembley next month, stop. New par— (*To* ANDERSON.)
Yes? (*Into phone.*) You can bank on it.

ANDERSON: I'm next door.

GRAYSON: (*Into phone*) —bank on it. New par— (*To* ANDERSON.)
Look, can you come back? (*Into phone.*) But for some
determined saving by third-choice Jim Bart in the injury
hyphen jinxed England goal, we would have been overdrawn
by four more when the books were closed, stop. Maybe
Napoleon was wrong when he said we were a nation of
shopkeepers, stop. Today England looked like a nation of
goalkeepers, stop. Davey, Petherbridge and Shell all made
saves on the line. New par.

ANDERSON: Do you mind if I listen—I missed the match.
(GRAYSON *waves him to a chair.* ANDERSON *sits on a chair next
to a door which is in fact a connecting door into the next room.
Not* ANDERSON'*s own room but the room on the other side of*
GRAYSON'*s room.*)

GRAYSON: (*Into phone*) Dickenson and Pratt were mostly left
standing by Wolker, with a W, and Deml, D dog, E
Edward, M mother, L London—who could go round the
halls as a telepathy act, stop. Only Crisp looked as if he had
a future outside Madame Tussaud's—a.u.d.s.—stop. He laid
on the two best chances, comma, both wasted by Pratt who
skied one and stubbed his toe on the other, stop. Crisp's,
apostrophe s. comment from where I was sitting looked salt
and vinegar flavoured . . .
(ANDERSON *has become aware that another voice is cutting in
from the next room. The door between the two rooms is not
quite closed. During* GRAYSON'*s last speech* ANDERSON *gently
pushes open the door and looks behind him and realizes that a
colleague of* GRAYSON'*s is also dictating in the next room.*
ANDERSON *stands up and looks into the next room and is drawn
into it by the rival report.*
This room belongs to CHAMBERLAIN.
Interior CHAMBERLAIN'*s room.* CHAMBERLAIN *on phone.*)

CHAMBERLAIN: Wilson, who would like to be thought the big bad
man of the English defence merely looked slow-footed and
slow-witted stop. Deml—D.E.M. mother L.—Deml got
round him five times on the trot, bracket, literally, close

bracket, using the same swerve, comma, making Wilson look elephantine in everything but memory, stop. On the fifth occasion there was nothing to prevent Deml scoring except what Broadbent took it on himself to do, which was to scythe Deml down from behind, stop. Halas scored from the penalty, stop.

(ANDERSON *sighs and sits down on the equivalent chair in* CHAMBERLAIN's *room.* CHAMBERLAIN *sees him.*)

Can I help you—?

ANDERSON: Sorry—I'm from next door.

CHAMBERLAIN: (*Into phone*) New paragraph— (*To* ANDERSON.) I won't be long— (*Into phone.*) This goal emboldened the Czechs to move Bartok, like the composer, forward and risk the consequences, stop. Ten minutes later, just before half time, comma, he was the man left over to collect a short corner from Halas and it was his chip which Jirasek rose to meet for a simple goal at the far post—

ANDERSON: I knew it!

(CHAMBERLAIN *turns to look at him.*)

CHAMBERLAIN: (*Into phone*) New paragraph. As with tragic opera, things got worse after the interval . . .

(ANDERSON *has stood up to leave. He leaves through* GRAYSON'S *room.* GRAYSON *is on the phone saying:*)

GRAYSON: (*Into the phone*) . . . Jirasek, unmarked at the far post, flapped into the air like a great stork, and rising a yard higher than Bart's outstretched hands, he put Czechoslovakia on the road to victory.

(ANDERSON *leaves the room without looking at* GRAYSON *or being noticed.*)

8. INT. HOTEL DINING ROOM

The cut is to gay Czech music.

The dining room has a stage. A small group of Czech musicians and singers in the tourist version of peasant costume is performing.

It is evening. At one of the tables STONE, *the American, and a* FRENCH-MAN *are sitting next to each other and sharing the table are* ANDERSON, MCKENDRICK *and* CHETWYN. *The three of them are, for different reasons, subdued.* STONE *is unsubdued. They are reaching the end of the meal.*

75

STONE: Hell's bells. Don't you understand English? When I say to you, 'Tell me what you mean,' you can only reply, 'I would wish to say so and so.' 'Never mind what you would wish to say,' I reply. 'Tell me what you *mean*.'

FRENCHMAN: Mais oui, but if you ask me in French, you must say, 'Qu'est-ce que vous voulez dire?'—'What is that which you wish to say?' Naturellement, it is in order for me to reply, 'Je veux dire etcetera.'

STONE: (*Excitedly*) But you are making *my* point—don't you see?

MCKENDRICK: What do you think the chances are of meeting a free and easy woman in a place like this?

STONE: I *can't* ask you in French.

MCKENDRICK: I don't mean free, necessarily.

FRENCHMAN: Pourquoi non? Qu'est-ce que vous voulez dire? Voila!—now I have asked you.

CHETWYN: You don't often see goose on an English menu. (CHETWYN *is the last to finish his main course. They have all eaten the main course. There are drinks and cups of coffee on the table.*)

STONE: The French have no verb meaning 'I mean'.

CHETWYN: Why's that I wonder.

STONE: They just don't.

CHETWYN: People are always eating goose in Dickens.

MCKENDRICK: Do you think it will be safe?

FRENCHMAN: Par exemple. Je vous dis, 'Qu'est-ce que vous voulez dire?'

MCKENDRICK: I mean one wouldn't want to be photographed through a two-way mirror.

STONE: I don't want to ask you what you would wish to say. I want to ask you what you *mean*. Let's assume there is a difference.

ANDERSON: We do have goose liver. What do they do with the rest of the goose?

STONE: Now assume that you say one but mean the other.

FRENCHMAN: Je dis quelque chose, mais je veux dire—

STONE: Right.

MCKENDRICK: (*To* STONE) Excuse me, Brad.

STONE: Yes?

MCKENDRICK: You eat well but you're a lousy eater.

(*This is a fair comment.* STONE *has spoken with his mouth full of bread, cake, coffee, etc., and he is generally messy about it.* STONE *smiles forgivingly but hardly pauses.*)

STONE: Excuse us.

FRENCHMAN: A bientôt.

(STONE *and the* FRENCHMAN *get up to leave.*)

STONE: (*Leaving*) You see, what you've got is an incorrect statement which when corrected looks like itself.

(*There is a pause.*)

MCKENDRICK: Did you have a chance to read my paper?

ANDERSON: I only had time to glance at it. I look forward to reading it carefully.

CHETWYN: I read it.

ANDERSON: Weren't you there for it?

MCKENDRICK: No, he sloped off for the afternoon.

ANDERSON: Well, you sly devil, Chetwyn. I bet you had a depressing afternoon. It makes the heart sick, doesn't it.

CHETWYN: Yes, it does rather. We don't know we've been born.

MCKENDRICK: He wasn't at the football match.

CHETWYN: Oh—is that where you were?

ANDERSON: No, I got distracted.

MCKENDRICK: He's being mysterious. I think it's a woman.

ANDERSON: (*To* CHETWYN) What were you doing?

CHETWYN: I was meeting some friends.

MCKENDRICK: He's being mysterious. I don't think it's a woman.

CHETWYN: I have friends here, that's all.

ANDERSON: (*To* MCKENDRICK) Was your paper well received?

MCKENDRICK: No. They didn't get it. I could tell from the questions that there'd been some kind of communications failure.

ANDERSON: The translation phones?

MCKENDRICK: No, no—they simply didn't understand the line of argument. Most of them had never heard of catastrophe theory, so they weren't ready for what is admittedly an audacious application of it.

ANDERSON: I must admit I'm not absolutely clear about it.

MCKENDRICK: It's like a reverse gear—no—it's like a breaking point. The mistake that people make is, they think a moral principle is indefinitely extendible, that it holds good for any

77

situation, a straight line cutting across the graph of our actual situation—here you are, you see— (*He uses a knife to score a line in front of him straight across the table cloth, left to right in front of him.*) 'Morality' down there; running parallel to 'Immorality' up here— (*He scores a parallel line.*) —and never the twain shall meet. They think that is what a principle means.

ANDERSON: And isn't it?

MCKENDRICK: No. The two lines are on the same plane. (*He holds out his flat hand, palm down, above the scored lines.*) They're the edges of the same plane—it's in three dimensions, you see—and if you twist the plane in a certain way, into what we call the catastrophe curve, you get a model of the sort of behaviour we find in the real world. There's a point—the catastrophe point—where your progress along one line of behaviour jumps you into the opposite line; the principle reverses itself at the point where a rational man would abandon it.

CHETWYN: Then it's not a principle.

MCKENDRICK: There aren't any principles in your sense. There are only a lot of principled people trying to behave as if there were.

ANDERSON: That's the same thing, surely.

MCKENDRICK: You're a worse case than Chetwyn and his primitive Greeks. At least he has the excuse of *believing* in goodness and beauty. You know they're fictions but you're so hung up on them you want to treat them as if they were God-given absolutes.

ANDERSON: I don't see how else they would have any practical value—

MCKENDRICK: So you end up using a moral principle as your excuse for acting against a moral interest. It's a sort of funk—

(ANDERSON, *under pressure, slams his cup back on to its saucer in a very uncharacteristic and surprising way. His anger is all the more alarming for that.*)

ANDERSON: You make your points altogether too easily, McKendrick. What need have you of moral courage when your principles reverse themselves so conveniently?

MCKENDRICK: All right! I've gone too far. As usual. Sorry. Let's talk about something else. There's quite an attractive woman hanging about outside, loitering in the vestibule.
(*The dining room door offers a view of the lobby.*)
Do you think it is a trap? My wife said to me—now, Bill, don't do anything daft, you know what you're like, if a blonde knocked on your door with the top three buttons of her police uniform undone and asked for a cup of sugar you'd convince yourself she was a bus conductress brewing up in the next room.

ANDERSON: (*Chastened*) I'm sorry . . . you're right up to a point. There would be no moral dilemmas if moral principles worked in straight lines and never crossed each other. One meets test situations which have troubled much cleverer men than us.

CHETWYN: A good rule, I find, is to try them out on men much *less* clever than us. I often ask my son what *he* thinks.

ANDERSON: Your son?

CHETWYN: Yes. He's eight.

MCKENDRICK: She's definitely glancing this way—seriously, do you think one could chat her up?
(ANDERSON *turns round to look through the door and we see now that the woman is* MRS HOLLAR.)

ANDERSON: Excuse me.
(*He gets up and starts to leave but then comes back immediately and takes his briefcase from under the table and then leaves. We stay with the table.* MCKENDRICK *watches* ANDERSON *meet* MRS HOLLAR *and shake her hand and they disappear.*)

MCKENDRICK: Bloody hell, it *was* a woman. Crafty old beggar.

9. EXT. STREET. NIGHT

ANDERSON *and* MRS HOLLAR *walking.*
A park. A park bench. SACHA HOLLAR *sitting on the bench.* ANDERSON *and* MRS HOLLAR *arrive.*

MRS HOLLAR: (*In Czech*) Here he is. (*To* ANDERSON.) Sacha. (*In Czech.*) Thank him for coming.

SACHA: She is saying thank you that you come.

MRS HOLLAR: (*In Czech*) We're sorry to bother him.

79

SACHA: She is saying sorry for the trouble.

ANDERSON: No, no I am sorry about . . . everything. Do you learn English at school?

SACHA: Yes. I am learning English two years. With my father also.

ANDERSON: You are very good.

SACHA: Not good. You are a friend of my father. Thank you.

ANDERSON: I'm afraid I've done nothing.

SACHA: You have his writing?

ANDERSON: His thesis? Yes. It's in here. (*He indicates his briefcase.*)

SACHA: (*In Czech*) It's all right, he's still got it.
(MRS HOLLAR *nods.*)

MRS HOLLAR: (*In Czech*) Tell him I didn't know who he was today.

SACHA: My mother is not knowing who you are, tomorrow at the apartment.

ANDERSON: Today.

SACHA: Today. Pardon. So she is saying, 'Come here! Come here! Come inside the apartment!' Because she is not knowing. My father is not telling her. He is telling me only.

ANDERSON: I see. What did he tell you?

SACHA: He will go see his friend the English professor. He is taking the writing.

ANDERSON: I see. Did he return home last night?

SACHA: No. He is arrested outside hotel. Then in the night they come to make search.

ANDERSON: Had they been there all night?

SACHA: At eleven o'clock they are coming. They search twenty hours.

ANDERSON: My God.

SACHA: In morning I go to Bartolomesskaya to be seeing him.

MRS HOLLAR: (*Explains*) Police.

SACHA: But I am not seeing him. They say go home. I am waiting. Then I am going home. Then I am seeing you.

ANDERSON: What were they looking for?

SACHA: (*Shrugs*) Western books. Also my father is writing things. Letters, politics, philosophy. They find nothing. Some English books they don't like but really nothing. But the dollars, of course, they pretend to find.

(MRS HOLLAR *hears the word dollars.*)

MRS HOLLAR: (*In Czech*) Tell him the dollars were put there by the police.

SACHA: Not my father's dollars. He is having no monies.

ANDERSON: Yes. I know.

SACHA: They must arrest him for dollars because he does nothing. No bad things. He is signing something. So they are making trouble.

ANDERSON: Yes.

MRS HOLLAR: (*In Czech*) Tell him about Jan.

SACHA: You must give back my father's thesis. Not now. The next days. My mother cannot take it.

ANDERSON: He asked me to take it to England.

SACHA: Not possible now. But thank you.

ANDERSON: He asked me to take it.

SACHA: Not possible. Now they search you, I think. At the aeroport. Because they are seeing you coming to the apartment and you have too much contact. Maybe they are seeing us now.

(ANDERSON *looks around him.*)

Is possible.

ANDERSON: (*Uncomfortably*) I ought to tell you . . . (*Quickly.*) I came to the apartment to give the thesis back. I refused him. But he was afraid he might be stopped—I thought he just meant searched, not arrested—

SACHA: Too quick—too quick—

(*Pause.*)

ANDERSON: What do you want me to do?

SACHA: My father's friend—he is coming to Philosophy Congress today.

ANDERSON: Tomorrow.

SACHA: Yes tomorrow. You give him the writing. Is called Jan. Is O.K. Good friend.

(ANDERSON *nods.*)

ANDERSON: Jan.

SACHA: (*In Czech*) He'll bring it to the university hall for Jan tomorrow. (SACHA *stands up.*) We go home now.

(MRS HOLLAR *gets up and shakes hands with* ANDERSON.)

ANDERSON: I'm sorry . . . What will happen to him?

MRS HOLLAR: (*In Czech*) What was that?

SACHA: (*In Czech*) He wants to know what will happen to Daddy.

MRS HOLLAR: Ruzyne.

SACHA: That is the prison. Ruzyne.

> (*Pause.*)

ANDERSON: I will, of course, try to help in England. I'll write
letters. The Czech Ambassador . . . I have friends, too, in
our government—

> (ANDERSON *realizes that the boy has started to cry. He is
> specially taken aback because he has been talking to him like an
> adult.*)

Now listen—I am personally friendly with important people
—the Minister of Education—people like that.

MRS HOLLAR: (*In Czech but to* ANDERSON) Please help Pavel—

ANDERSON: Mrs Hollar—I will do everything I can for him.

> (*He watches* MRS HOLLAR *and* SACHA *walk away into the dark.*)

10. INT. ANDERSON'S ROOM. NIGHT

ANDERSON *is lying fully dressed on the bed. His eyes open. Only light
from the window. There are faint voices from* GRAYSON'S *room. After
a while* ANDERSON *gets up and leaves his room and knocks on* GRAYSON'S
door.

Exterior GRAYSON'S *room.*

GRAYSON *opens his door.*

GRAYSON: Oh hello. Sorry, are we making too much noise?

ANDERSON: No, it's all right, but I heard you were still up and I
wondered if I could ask a favour of you. I wonder if I
could borrow your typewriter.

GRAYSON: My typewriter?

ANDERSON: Yes.

GRAYSON: Well, I'm leaving in the morning.

ANDERSON: I'll let you have it back first thing. I'm leaving on the
afternoon plane myself.

GRAYSON: Oh—all right then.

ANDERSON: That's most kind.

> (*During the above the voices from the room have been semi-
> audible.*
>
> MCKENDRICK'S *voice, rather drunk, but articulate, is heard.*)

MCKENDRICK: (*His voice only, heard underneath the above dialogue*)
Now, listen to me, I'm a professional philosopher. You'll do
well to listen to what I have to say.

ANDERSON: That sounds as if you've got McKendrick in there.

GRAYSON: Oh—is he one of yours?

ANDERSON: I wouldn't put it like that.

GRAYSON: He's getting as tight as a tick.

ANDERSON: Yes.

GRAYSON: You couldn't collect him, could you? He's going to get
clouted in a minute.

ANDERSON: Go ahead and clout him, if you like.

GRAYSON: It's not me. It's Broadbent and a couple of the lads.
Your pal sort of latched on to us in the bar. He really ought
to be getting home.

ANDERSON: I'll see what I can do.

(ANDERSON *follows* GRAYSON *into the room.*)

MCKENDRICK: How can you expect the kids to be little gentlemen
when their heroes behave like yobs—answer me that—no—
you haven't answered my question—if you've got yobs on
the fields you're going to have yobs on the terraces.

(*Interior* GRAYSON's *room.*

MCKENDRICK *is the only person standing up. He is holding
court, with a bottle of whisky in one hand and his glass in the
other. Around this small room are* BROADBENT, CRISP,
CHAMBERLAIN, *and perhaps one or two members of the England
squad. Signs of a bottle party.*)

GRAYSON: (*Closing his door*) I thought philosophers were quiet,
studious sort of people.

ANDERSON: Well, some of us are.

MCKENDRICK: (*Shouts*) Anderson! You're the very man I want to
see! We're having a philosophical discussion about the
yob ethics of professional footballers—

BROADBENT: You want to watch it, mate.

MCKENDRICK: Roy here is sensitive because he gave away a
penalty today, by a deliberate foul. To stop a certain goal he
hacked a chap down. After all, a penalty might be saved and
broken legs are quite rare—

(BROADBENT *stands up but* MCKENDRICK *pacifies him with a
gesture.*)

it's perfectly all right—you were adopting the utilitarian values of the game, for the good of the team, for England! But I'm not talking about particular acts of expediency. No, I'm talking about the whole *ethos*.

ANDERSON: McKendrick, don't you think, it's about time we retired?

MCKENDRICK: (*Ignoring him*) Now, I've played soccer for years. Years and *years*. I played soccer from the age of *eight* until I was *thirteen*. At which point I went to a rugger school. Even so, Tommy here will tell you that I still consider myself something of a left winger. (*This is to* CRISP.) Sorry about that business in the lift, by the way, Tommy. Well, one thing I remember clearly from my years and *years* of soccer is that if two players go for a ball which then goes into touch, there's never any doubt *among those players* which of them touched the ball last. I can't remember one occasion in all those years and *years* when the player who touched the ball last didn't realize it. So, what I want to know *is*—why is it that on Match of the Day, every time the bloody ball goes into touch, *both* players claim the throw-in for their own side? I merely ask for information. Is it because they are very, very stupid or is it because a dishonest advantage is as welcome as an honest one?

CHAMBERLAIN: Well, look, it's been a long evening, old chap—

ANDERSON: Tomorrow is another day, McKendrick.

MCKENDRICK: Tomorrow, in my experience, is usually the same day. Have a drink—

ANDERSON: No thank you.

MCKENDRICK: Here's a question for anthropologists. Name me a tribe which organizes itself into teams for sporting encounters and greets every score against their opponents with paroxysms of childish glee, whooping, dancing and embracing in an ecstasy of crowing self-congratulation in the very midst of their disconsolate fellows?—Who are these primitives who pile all their responses into the immediate sensation, unaware or uncaring of the long undulations of life's fortunes? Yes, you've got it! (*He chants the Match of the Day signature tune.*) It's the yob-of-the-month competition, entries on a postcard please. But the question is—is it because they're working class, or is it because financial greed has corrupted them? Or is it both?

ANDERSON: McKendrick, you are being offensive.

MCKENDRICK: Anderson is one of life's cricketers. Clap, clap. (*He claps in a well-bred sort of way and puts on a well-bred voice.*) Well played, sir. Bad luck, old chap. The comparison with cricket may suggest to you that yob ethics are working class.

(BROADBENT *comes up to* MCKENDRICK *and pushes him against the wall.* MCKENDRICK *is completely unconcerned, escapes and continues without pause.*)

But you would be quite wrong. Let me refer you to a typical rugby team of Welsh miners. A score is acknowledged with pride but with restraint, the scorer himself composing his features into an expressionless mask lest he might be suspected of exulting in his opponents' misfortune—my God, it does the heart good, doesn't it? I conclude that yob ethics are caused by financial greed.

ANDERSON: Don't be such an ass.

(MCKENDRICK *takes this as an intellectual objection.*)

MCKENDRICK: You think it's the adulation, perhaps? (*To* CRISP.) Is it the adulation, Tommy, which has corrupted you?

CRISP: What's he flaming on about?

CHAMBERLAIN: Well I think it's time for my shut-eye.

CRISP: No, I want to know what he's saying about me. He's giving me the needle.

ANDERSON: (*To* MCKENDRICK) May I remind you that you profess to be something of a pragmatist yourself in matters of ethics—

MCKENDRICK: Ah yes—I see—you think that because I don't believe in reliable signposts on the yellow brick road to rainbowland, you think I'm a bit of a yob myself—the swift kick in the kneecap on the way up the academic ladder —the Roy Broadbent of Stoke— (*To* BROADBENT.) Stoke's my team, you know.

BROADBENT: Will you tell this stupid bugger his philosophy is getting up my nostrils.

GRAYSON: You're not making much sense, old boy.

MCKENDRICK: Ah! Grayson here has a fine logical mind. He has

85

put his finger on the flaw in my argument, namely that the reason footballers are yobs may be nothing to do with being working class, or with financial greed, or with adulation, or even with being footballers. It may be simply that football attracts a certain kind of person, namely yobs—

(*This is as far as he gets when* BROADBENT *smashes him in the face.* MCKENDRICK *drops.*)

CRISP: Good on you, Roy.

(ANDERSON *goes to* MCKENDRICK *who is flat on the floor.*)

ANDERSON: McKendrick . . .

CHAMBERLAIN: Well, I'm going to bed.

(CHAMBERLAIN *goes through the connecting door into his own room and closes the door.*)

BROADBENT: He can't say that sort of thing and get away with it.

GRAYSON: Where's his room?

ANDERSON: On the third floor.

GRAYSON: Bloody hell.

CRISP: He's waking up.

BROADBENT: He's all right.

ANDERSON: Come on McKendrick.

(*They all lift* MCKENDRICK *to his feet.* MCKENDRICK *makes no protest. He's just about able to walk.*)

I'll take him down in the lift. (*He sees the typewriter in its case and says to* GRAYSON.) I'll come back for the typewriter. (*He leads* MCKENDRICK *towards the door.*)

MCKENDRICK: (*Mutters*) All right. I went too far. Let's talk about something else.

(*But* MCKENDRICK *keeps walking or staggering.* ANDERSON *opens* GRAYSON'S *door.*)

BROADBENT: Here. That bloody Jirasek. Just like you said.

ANDERSON: Yes.

BROADBENT: They don't teach you nothing at that place then.

ANDERSON: No.

(ANDERSON *helps* MCKENDRICK *out and closes the door.*)

11. THE COLLOQUIUM

ANDERSON *comes to the lectern. There is a Czech* CHAIRMAN *behind him.*

CHETWYN *is in the audience but* MCKENDRICK *is not. We arrive as*

ANDERSON *approaches the microphone.* ANDERSON *lays a sheaf of typewritten paper on the lectern.*

ANDERSON: I propose in this paper to take up a problem which many have taken up before me, namely the conflict between the rights of individuals and the rights of the community. I will be making a distinction between rights and rules.

(*We note that the* CHAIRMAN, *listening politely and intently, is suddenly puzzled. He himself has some papers and from these he extracts one, which is in fact the official copy of* ANDERSON's *official paper. He starts looking at it. It doesn't take him long to satisfy himself that* ANDERSON *is giving a different paper. These things happen while* ANDERSON *speaks. At the same time the three* INTERPRETERS *in their booths, while speaking into their microphones as* ANDERSON *speaks, are also in some difficulty because they have copies of* ANDERSON's *official paper.*)

I will seek to show that rules, in so far as they are related to rights, are a secondary and consequential elaboration of primary rights, and I will be associating rules generally with communities and rights generally with individuals. I will seek to show that a conflict between the two is generally a pseudo-conflict arising out of one side or the other pressing a pseudo-right. Although claiming priority for rights over rules—where they are in conflict—I will be defining rights as fictions acting as incentives to the adoption of practical values; and I will further propose that although these rights are fictions there is an obligation to treat them as if they were truths; and further, that although this obligation can be shown to be based on values which are based on fictions, there is an obligation to treat *that* obligation as though it were based on truth; and so on *ad infinitum.*

(*At this point the* CHAIRMAN *interrupts him.*)

CHAIRMAN: Pardon me—Professor—this is not your paper—

ANDERSON: In what sense? I am indisputably giving it.

CHAIRMAN: But it is not the paper you were invited to give.

ANDERSON: I wasn't invited to give a particular paper.

CHAIRMAN: You offered one.

ANDERSON: That's true.

CHAIRMAN: But this is not it.

ANDERSON: No. I changed my mind.

CHAIRMAN: But it is irregular.

ANDERSON: I didn't realize it mattered.

CHAIRMAN: It is a discourtesy.

ANDERSON: (*Taken aback*) Bad manners? I am sorry.

CHAIRMAN: You cannot give this paper. We do not have copies.

ANDERSON: Do you mean that philosophical papers require some sort of clearance?

CHAIRMAN: The interpreters cannot work without copies.

ANDERSON: Don't worry. It is not a technical paper. I will speak a little slower if you like. (ANDERSON *turns back to the microphone*.) If we decline to define rights as fictions, albeit with the force of truths, there are only two senses in which humans could be said to have rights. Firstly, humans might be said to have certain rights if they had collectively and mutually agreed to give each other these rights. This would merely mean that humanity is a rather large club with club rules, but it is not what is generally meant by human rights. It is not what Locke meant, and it is not what the American Founding Fathers meant when, taking the hint from Locke, they held certain rights to be unalienable—among them, life, liberty and the pursuit of happiness. The early Americans claimed these as the endowment of God—which is the *second* sense in which humans might be said to have rights. This is a view more encouraged in some communities than in others. I do not wish to dwell on it here except to say that it *is* a view and not a deduction, and that I do not hold it myself.

What strikes us is the consensus about an individual's rights put forward both by those who invoke God's authority and by those who invoke no authority at all other than their own idea of what is fair and sensible. The first Article of the American Constitution, guaranteeing freedom of religious observance, of expression, of the press, and of assembly, is closely echoed by Articles 28 and 32 of the no less admirable Constitution of Czechoslovakia, our generous hosts on this occasion. Likewise, protection from invasion of privacy, from unreasonable search and from interference with letters and correspondence guaranteed to the American people by Article 4 is likewise guaranteed to the Czech people by

Article 31.

(*The* CHAIRMAN, *who has been more and more uncomfortable,
leaves the stage at this point. He goes into the 'wings'. At some
distance from* ANDERSON, *but still just in earshot of* ANDERSON,
i.e. one can hear ANDERSON'*s words clearly if faintly, is a
telephone. Perhaps in a stage manager's office. We go with the*
CHAIRMAN *but we can still hear* ANDERSON.)

Is such a consensus remarkable? Not at all. If there is a
God, we his creations would doubtless subscribe to his
values. And if there is not a God, he, our creation, would
undoubtedly be credited with values which we think to be
fair and sensible. But what is fairness? What is sense? What
are these values which we take to be self-evident? And why
are they values?

12. INT. MCKENDRICK'S ROOM

MCKENDRICK *is fully dressed and coming round from a severe hangover.
His room is untidier than* ANDERSON'*s. Clothes are strewn about. His
suitcase, half full, is open. His briefcase is also in evidence.* MCKEN-
DRICK *looks at his watch, but it has stopped. He goes to the telephone
and dials.*

13. INT. ANDERSON'S ROOM

*The phone starts to ring. The camera pulls back from the phone and
we see that there are two men in the room, plainclothes* POLICEMEN,
*searching the room. They look at the phone but only for a moment, and
while it rings they continue quietly. They search the room very
discreetly. We see one carefully slide open a drawer and we cut away.*

14. THE COLLOQUIUM

We have returned to ANDERSON'*s paper. There is no* CHAIRMAN *on
stage.*

ANDERSON: Ethics were once regarded as a sort of monument, a
ghostly Eiffel Tower constructed of Platonic entities like
honesty, loyalty, fairness, and so on, all bolted together and
consistent with each other, harmoniously stressed so as to
keep the edifice standing up: an ideal against which we
measured our behaviour. The tower has long been demolished.
In our own time linguistic philosophy proposes that the

notion of, say, justice has no existence outside the ways in which we choose to employ the word, and indeed *consists* only of the way in which we employ it. In other words, that ethics are not the inspiration of our behaviour but merely the creation of our utterances.

(*Over the latter part of this we have gone back to the* CHAIRMAN *who is on the telephone. The* CHAIRMAN *is doing little talking and some listening.*)

And yet common observation shows us that this view demands qualification. A small child who cries 'that's not fair' when punished for something done by his brother or sister is apparently appealing to an idea of justice which is, for want of a better word, natural. And we must see that natural justice, however illusory, does inspire many people's behaviour much of the time. As an ethical utterance it seems to be an attempt to define a sense of rightness which is not simply derived from some other utterance elsewhere.

(*We cut now to a backstage area, but* ANDERSON's *voice is continuous, heard through the sort of P.A. system which one finds backstage at theatres.*

The CHAIRMAN *hurries along the corridor, seeking, and now finding a uniformed* 'FIREMAN', *a backstage official. During this* ANDERSON *speaks.*)

Now a philosopher exploring the difficult terrain of right and wrong should not be over impressed by the argument 'a child would know the difference'. But when, let us say, we are being persuaded that it is ethical to put someone in prison for reading or writing the wrong books, it is well to be reminded that you can persuade a man to believe almost anything provided he is clever enough, but it is much more difficult to persuade someone less clever. There is a sense of right and wrong which precedes utterance. It is individually experienced and it concerns one person's dealings with another person. From this experience we have built a system of ethics which is the sum of individual acts of recognition of individual right.

(*During this we have returned to* ANDERSON *in person. And at this point the* CHAIRMAN *re-enters the stage and goes and sits in his chair.* ANDERSON *continues, ignoring him.*)

If this is so, the implications are serious for a collective or State ethic which finds itself in conflict with individual rights, and seeks, in the name of the people, to impose its values on the very individuals who comprise the State. The illogic of this manoeuvre is an embarrassment to totalitarian systems. An attempt is sometimes made to answer it by consigning the whole argument to 'bourgeois logic', which is a concept no easier to grasp than bourgeois physics or bourgeois astronomy. No, the fallacy must lie elsewhere—
(*At this point loud bells, electric bells, ring. The fire alarm. The* CHAIRMAN *leaps up and shouts.*)

CHAIRMAN: (*In Czech*) Don't panic! There appears to be a fire. Please leave the hall in an orderly manner. (*In English.*) Fire! Please leave quietly!
(*The philosophers get to their feet and start heading for the exit.* ANDERSON *calmly gathers his papers up and leaves the stage.*)

15. INT. AIRPORT

People leaving the country have to go through a baggage check. There are at least three separate but adjacent benches at which customs men and women search the baggage of travellers. The situation here is as follows:

At the first bench CHETWYN *is in mid-search.*

At the second bench ANDERSON *is in mid-search.*

At the third bench a traveller is in mid-search.

There is a short queue of people waiting for each bench. The leading man in the queue waiting for the third bench is MCKENDRICK. *The search at this third bench is cursory.*

However, ANDERSON *is being searched very thoroughly. We begin on* ANDERSON. *We have not yet noted* CHETWYN.

At ANDERSON's *bench a uniformed customs* WOMAN *is examining the contents of his suitcase, helped by a uniformed customs* MAN. *At the same time a plainclothes* POLICEMAN *is very carefully searching everything in* ANDERSON's *briefcase.*

We see the customs MAN *take a cellophane wrapped box of chocolates from* ANDERSON's *case. He strips off the cellophane and looks at the chocolates and then he digs down to look at the second layer of chocolates.* ANDERSON *watches this with amazement. The chocolate box is closed and put back in the case. Meanwhile a nest of wooden*

*dolls, the kind in which one doll fits inside another, is reduced to its
components.*

The camera moves to find MCKENDRICK *arriving at the third desk.
There is no plainclothes man there. The customs* OFFICER *there opens
his briefcase and flips, in a rather cursory way, through* MCKENDRICK'S
papers. He asks MCKENDRICK *to open his case. He digs about for a
moment in* MCKENDRICK'S *case.*

Back at ANDERSON'S *bench the plainclothes* MAN *is taking* ANDERSON'S
wallet from ANDERSON'S *hand. He goes through every piece of paper
in the wallet.*

We go back to MCKENDRICK'S *bench to find* MCKENDRICK *closing his
case and being moved on.* MCKENDRICK *turns round to* ANDERSON *to
speak.*

MCKENDRICK: You picked the wrong queue, old man. Russian
    roulette. And Chetwyn.
    (*We now discover* CHETWYN *who is going through a similar
    search to* ANDERSON'S. *He has a plainclothes* MAN *too. This* MAN
    is looking down the spine of a book from CHETWYN'S *suitcase.
    We now return to* ANDERSON'S *bench. We find that the customs
    MAN has discovered a suspicious bulge in the zipped compartment
    on the underside of the lid of* ANDERSON'S *suitcase.* ANDERSON'S
    face tells us that he has a spasm of anxiety. The bulge suggests
    something about the size of* HOLLAR'S *envelope. The customs
    MAN zips open the compartment and extracts the copy of
    MCKENDRICK'S girly magazine.* ANDERSON *is embarrassed.
    We return to* CHETWYN *whose briefcase is being searched paper
    by paper. The customs* OFFICIAL *searching his suitcase finds a
    laundered shirt, nicely ironed and folded. He opens the shirt
    up and discovers about half a dozen sheets of writing-paper.
    Thin paper with typewriting on it. Also a photograph of a man.
    The plainclothes* MAN *joins the customs* OFFICIAL *and he starts
    looking at these pieces of paper. He looks up at* CHETWYN
    whose face has gone white.*)

16. INT. AEROPLANE
The plane is taxiing.
MCKENDRICK *and* ANDERSON *are sitting together.*
MCKENDRICK *looks shocked.*
MCKENDRICK: Silly bugger. Honestly.

ANDERSON: It's all right—they'll put him on the next plane.

MCKENDRICK: To Siberia.

ANDERSON: No, no, don't be ridiculous. It wouldn't look well for them, would it? All the publicity. I don't think there's anything in Czech law about being in possession of letters to Amnesty International and the U.N. and that sort of thing. They couldn't treat Chetwyn as though he were a Czech national anyway.

MCKENDRICK: Very unpleasant for him though.

ANDERSON: Yes.

MCKENDRICK: He took a big risk.

ANDERSON: Yes.

MCKENDRICK: I wouldn't do it. Would you?

ANDERSON: No. He should have known he'd be searched.

MCKENDRICK: Why did they search you?

ANDERSON: They thought I might have something.

MCKENDRICK: Did you have anything?

ANDERSON: I did in a way.

MCKENDRICK: What was it?

ANDERSON: A thesis. Apparently rather slanderous from the State's point of view.

MCKENDRICK: Where did you hide it?

ANDERSON: In your briefcase.

(*Pause.*)

MCKENDRICK: You what?

ANDERSON: Last night. I'm afraid I reversed a principle.

(MCKENDRICK *opens his briefcase and finds* HOLLAR's *envelope.* ANDERSON *takes it from him.* MCKENDRICK *is furious.*)

MCKENDRICK: You utter bastard.

ANDERSON: I thought you would approve.

MCKENDRICK: Don't get clever with me. (*He relapses, shaking.*) Jesus. It's not quite playing the game is it?

ANDERSON: No, I suppose not. But they were very unlikely to search *you.*

MCKENDRICK: That's not the bloody point.

ANDERSON: I thought it was. But you could be right. Ethics is a very complicated business. That's why they have these congresses.

(*The plane picks up speed on the runway towards take-off.*)